Arab Archery

AN ARABIC MANUSCRIPT OF ABOUT A. D. 1500 "A BOOK ON THE EXCELLENCE OF THE BOW & ARROW" AND THE DESCRIPTION THEREOF.

TRANSLATED AND EDITED BY

NABIH AMIN FARIS

AND ROBERT POTTER ELMER

Martino Publishing
Mansfield Centre, CT
2016

Martino Publishing
P.O. Box 373,
Mansfield Centre, CT 06250 USA

ISBN 978-1-61427-924-2

Cover Design Tiziana Matarazzo

Printed in the United States of America On 100% Acid-Free Paper

Arab Archery

AN ARABIC MANUSCRIPT OF ABOUT

A. D. 1500 "A BOOK ON THE EXCEL-

LENCE OF THE BOW & ARROW" AND

THE DESCRIPTION THEREOF.

TRANSLATED AND EDITED BY

NABIH AMIN FARIS

AND ROBERT POTTER ELMER

PRINCETON UNIVERSITY PRESS 1945

PRINCETON NEW JERSEY

Printed in the United States of America by
Princeton University Press, Princeton, New Jersey
London: Humphrey Milford
Oxford University Press

Drawings by Jeannette Atkins

PREFACE

THE translation and editing of this manuscript has been a joint enterprise undertaken by two men, one of whom started with great interest in Arabic studies and virtually no knowledge of archery, the other familiar with archery but without special training or experience in the Oriental field. We feel that each of us has helped expand the knowledge and interests of the other, and it is our hope that this book will be read by both kinds of readers, and with similar results.

In the Garrett Collection of Arabic Manuscripts in Princeton University Library is what appears to be a unique manuscript on archery. As works on sports in this collection are not numerous, this one attracted special attention. Faris thought of publishing the work but was dissuaded by his unfamiliarity with archery either in theory or practice. In 1940, however, he wrote an article on the Garrett Collection for the Princeton University Library *Chronicle*, and in the course of it referred casually to this manuscript. This article fell into the hands of Elmer, whose interest in archery is well known. He was so eager to have the work made available in English that he offered to supply the technical advice if Faris would do the translation.

We set about the task together, following a theoretical division of labor but actually carrying forward what in all truth proved to be a joint enterprise—for instance Elmer's technical knowledge frequently furnished the key to difficult linguistic problems, while Faris's reading of Arabic often gave the answer to technical questions that have intrigued and mystified students of archery for many years.

The manuscript itself comprises 353 pages, 19 x 13.5 cm., with a written surface of 13 x 8 cm. The paper is glazed European of the fifteenth century. Unfortunately the identity of the author remains unknown, although we know from references in the body of the manuscript that he was a North African from Morocco.

Almost the only source of detailed knowledge of early English archery is *Toxophilus, or the Schole of Shootynge*, which was written by Roger Ascham in 1542 and 1543 and was published in 1544. *Arab Archery* is nearly contemporary with that famous book—probably preceding it by a few years—and may be considered to be on an equal plane of merit. This ancient Arabic manuscript is the only treatise on the archery of the medieval Orient that has been translated into English. It is thorough and authoritative, evidently the work of an expert bowman. A vast amount of information concerning the long-range artillery, by which one eastern empire after another had been won, is here brought forth into full light after having lain hidden for centuries.

It could be used as a textbook on archery today.

NABIH AMIN FARIS
AND
ROBERT POTTER ELMER

CONTENTS

ILLUSTRATIONS

Arab Archery

KEY TO THE PRONUNCIATION OF ARABIC WORDS

ā like the a in car. ū like the u in rule.
ī like ee in feel.

A dot . under d (ḍ) broadens the vowel following; the same is true with the letters s, t, and z.

Z dotted (ẓ) corresponds to dh followed by a broad vowel.

H dotted (ḥ) represents a guttural not found in the English phonetic system.

' represents a glottal stop. Compare the *a* in German *alte*.

' represents a guttural not found in the English phonetic system.

Abu means father (of). Ibn means son (of).
Al- is the Arabic definite article.
Dhu (dhi in Dat. and Gen.) means possessor of, or he of.
Dhu-'l-Aktāf means "he of the shoulders."
Muḥammad (mo͝o.ḥăm'.măd)
Abu-Hurayrah (ă.bo͞o' ho͞o.rī'.răh) Uḥud (o͞o'.ḥo͞od')
Sa'd ibn-abi-Waqqās (să'd ĭbn ă.bē' wăq.qäs')
Abu-Ṭalḥah (ă.bo͞o' ṭăl'.ḥăh)
Qatādah ibn-al-Nu'mān (qă.tȧ'.dăh ĭbn ăn.no͞o'.mȧn')
Abu-al-Faḍl 'Iyāḍ (ă.bo͞ol' .făḍl 'ĭ.yăḍ')
Badr (bădr) 'Ali ('ă.lī' or 'ă.lē')
'Uqbah ĭbn-'Āmir ('o͞oq'.băh ĭbn 'ȧ'.mĭr)
Ḥijāz (ḥĭ.jȧz')
Abu-Hāshim al-Māwardi
(ă.bo͞o' hȧ'.shĭm ăl.mȧ'.war.dē')
Ṭahir al-Balkhi (ṭä'.hĭr ăl.băl.khē')
Isḥāq al-Raqqi (ĭs.ḥȧq' ăr.răq'.qĭ)
Al-Ṭabari (ăṭ.ṭă'.bă.rē')
Abu-Ja'far Muḥammad ibn-al-Ḥasan al-Harawi (ă.bo͞o' jă'.făr mo͝o.hăm'.măd ĭbn ăl.ḥă.săn' ăl.hă.ră.wē')
Sāpūr dhu-'l-Aktāf (sȧ'.po͞or' dho͞ol.ăk.tȧf')
'Ali ibn-abi-Ṭālib ('ă.lī' ĭbn ă.bē'. ṭä'.lĭb)
Bahrām Gūr (băh.rȧm' go͞or')
Ṣa'dīyah (ṣă'.dē'.yăh)
Abu-Muḥammad ibn-'Aṭīyah
(ă.bo͞o' mo͞o.hăm.măd' ĭbn 'ă.ṭē'.yăh)

A Book on the Excellence of the Bow and Arrow and the Description Thereof

I. In the Name of God the Merciful, the Compassionate

THERE is no way unto God but through Him, God alone. May the blessing of God be upon our Lord Muḥammad and upon His Family and Companions. Thanks be to God whose bounties upon His creatures are perfect and complete, and whose wisdom is evident in His creation throughout the world; who has made all without any previous pattern, and endued His work with utility; faultless and precious. He has made marksmanship the undoing of the enemy in war and, in raids, the means of victory over the foe; and has promised a high rank in Paradise to him who shoots an arrow in His cause, regardless of whether the archer fells an enemy or misses the mark.

I thank God for granting me mastery over the minute details of archery, and for giving me skill in its difficult technique; for its secrets which He has revealed unto me, and its mysteries which, through His grace, He unveiled to me. With His praise every matter of importance is commenced. And may the blessing of God be upon our Lord, Muḥammad, His prophet, for through invoking God's blessing upon him is every deed deduced and every statement formulated. I also thank God for His benefits and bounties which He grants unto us, even before we beseech His grace. Furthermore I testify that there is no god but God, He alone, no associates has He, and that

Muḥammad is His servant and apostle: a testimony of one aware of its necessity and cognizant of its obligation.

Holy War is one of the best forms of worship, and is obligatory upon every believer individually, though it has now become incumbent on the whole community collectively. Furthermore, the Holy Koran and the tradition have dwelt upon its excellence, thereby urging every Moslem to seek, through it, the martyr's crown. The Apostle of God said: "By him who holds in His palm Muḥammad's life, it is my desire to meet my end on the battleground of God, and be brought back to life, and die again, and again, and yet again." According to another version: "Would that I were given to die on the battleground of God, and be brought back to life, only to die again, and yet again, fighting His battles." Abu-Hurayrah was wont to say: "Of every single year, three months belong to God and His cause." The Prophet also said: "Of all the godly men who desire to be brought back to life, only the martyrs are granted their request." God also has enjoined us to prepare force against the polytheists in order to strike terror in their hearts, and pointed to us the excellence of the bow and arrow as implements of war. Thus He said: "Make ready against them what force ye can, and strong squadrons whereby ye may strike terror into the enemy of God and your enemy." In urging that force be made ready against the enemy, God has indicated the importance of drilling and training in the use of all implements of war, in order to acquire skill, gain proficiency, obtain adroitness, and develop facility in their use. Furthermore, the Apostle pointed out that of all the instruments of war, the bow and arrow are the most effective and the greatest.

The Prophet also said: "The hand of man has wielded no weapon which was not excelled by the bow." Is there anything more excellent than a man who has mastered marksmanship, who picks up his bow and showers the polytheists with his arrows? The crowds fear him, and the brave knights stand in awe before him. Many a weak city has been defended by a single archer, and many an army has been disbanded and scattered with a single arrow. During the battle of Uḥud, the Apostle addressed Sa'd ibn-abi-Waqqāṣ, abu-Ṭalḥah, and Qatādah ibn-al-Nu'mān, who stood by him defending him with their bows and arrows, while most of his Companions fled away: "Stand firm; victory shall remain ours so long as ye stand firm." Indeed this is a great tribute to the bow and arrow and a compliment for their service. He that wields them will most certainly be victorious. How then could a sane Moslem place his confidence in any other weapon, or dare face his adversary with any other instrument of war?

The poet said:

> Bows, with the strings of which victory is bound;
> In praise of their excellence the Scriptures resound.

Said another:

> If glory be to slay the foe,
> 'Tis best to use the fastest throw,
> And loose the arrow from the bow.

Furthermore, the bow and the arrow are the most effective and devastating of the instruments of war despite the fact that they are the least cumbersome to carry and use. Unfortunately, however, there are very few contemporaries who can use the Arab bow and fewer still who know anything about its methods and technique. For this reason I decided to write a book on marksmanship and the use of the Arab bow. Such a book I had, in fact, written and entitled it *Kifāyat al-Muqtaṣid al-Baṣīr fi al-Ramy 'an al-Qaws al-'Arabīyah bi-al-Sahm al-Ṭawīl w-al-Qaṣīr* [The Sufficiency of the Discerning Student: on Shooting with the Arab Bow with the Long Arrow and the Short]. It was, however, too brief, and the need for a detailed and comprehensive work on the subject was still felt. Consequently, I set out to fulfill this need. This book is the result. Verily God is my refuge and my trust.

II. On Holy War and the service of archery therein

HOLY WAR is to expend oneself in the way of God and to honor His Word which He has laid down as a path to Paradise and a highway leading thereto. Said He: "Do valiantly in the cause of God as it behooveth you to do for Him."

It is a duty, incumbent on the community of the believers collectively, to be carried out by some on behalf of the whole community. God said: "The faithful must not march forth all together to wars; and if a part of every band of them march not out, it is that they may instruct themselves in their religion." In other words, God has enjoined that some should march to battle for His cause, while others stay behind to keep the torch of His law burning. Said God again: "Those believers who sit at home free from trouble, and those who do valiantly in the cause of God with their substance and their persons, shall not be treated alike. God hath assigned to those who contend earnestly with their persons and with their substance a rank above that of those who sit at home. Goodly promises hath He made to all. But God hath assigned the strenuous a rich recompense, above that of those who sit at home: rank of His own bestowal, and forgiveness, and mercy; for God is Indulgent, Merciful." Furthermore, the Prophet embarked upon his wars and raids with but a few of his followers; he left some behind at home.

Others have maintained that Holy War was a duty obligatory upon every Moslem individually. In support of their position they cited the words of God when He said:

"Attack those who associate other gods with God in all, as they attack you in all." And again: "March ye forth the light and heavy armed, and contend with your substance and your persons in the Way of God. This, if ye know it, will be better for you." And still again: "War has been prescribed to you, but from it ye are averse."

At any rate, Holy War is among the best forms of worship and one of the most acceptable works of righteousness before God. Thus He said: "Verily God loveth those who, as though they were a solid wall, do battle for His cause in serried array. O ye who believe! Shall I show you a merchandise that shall deliver you from the sore torment? Believe in God and in His Apostle, and do valiantly in the cause of God with your wealth and your persons. This, did ye but know it, will be best for you. Your sins He will forgive you, and He will bring you into gardens beneath the shades of which rivers flow; into charming abodes in the gardens of Eden. This shall be the great bliss." God also said: "And repute not those slain in the path of God to be dead. Nay, alive with their Lord, are they richly sustained; rejoicing in what God of His bounty hath vouchsafed them; filled with joy for those who follow them, but have not overtaken them, that on them nor fear shall come, nor grief; filled with joy at the favors of God, and at His bounty, and that God suffereth not the reward of the faithful to perish." He also said: "Verily, of the faithful God hath bought their persons and their substance, on condition of Paradise for them in return; on the path of God shall they fight, and slay, and be slain. A promise for this is pledged in the Evangel, and in the Koran, and who is more faithful to his engagement than God? Rejoice, therefore, in the contract that ye have contracted; for this shall be the great bliss."

The Apostle of God, on being asked concerning the best acts of worship, replied: "Belief in God and Holy War in the cause of God." He also said: "Compared to Holy War, all the acts of worship put together are like a drop of water in the spacious sea." And again: "If I should spend the whole night in prayer and fast the entire day, I would not attain the stature of him who spends a day in Holy War." And again: "He who dies without having taken any part in Holy War, or without ever entertaining such an undertaking in his mind, is guilty of deceit and hypocrisy."

III. On the excellence of the Arab bow, its use, adoption, the reward of the maker of its arrows, its target, urging the mastery of its technique, the offense of him who discards it after he has learned its use, and the first to use and the first to make it

SAID GOD: "Make ready against them what force ye can." This was interpreted by the Apostle of God as marksmanship. The learned judge abu-al-Faḍl 'Iyāḍ, in appraising the different commentaries upon these passages, said that the Apostle of God had once declared: "The hand of man has not reached to an implement of war to which the bow and arrow are not superior." Said he again: "Use ye the spear and the Arab bow, for with them was your prophet victorious and with their might have ye conquered the earth."

Anas also related that never has the bow been mentioned before the Apostle of God except he said no weapon excelled it.

The Apostle said on another occasion that Gabriel approached him on the day of the Battle of Badr brandishing an Arab bow. And again when 'Ali appeared before him carrying an Arab bow, the Apostle exclaimed: "Thus hath Gabriel stood before me. O God, to him who seeketh therewith game for meat, give Thou sustenance, and to him who seeketh therewith Thine aid, give victory, and to him who seeketh therewith livelihood, give maintenance."

It was also related that whenever the Apostle mounted the pulpit to deliver a speech or a sermon, he used to lean against an Arab bow. It was also reported that he had used his bow until the *siyahs*[1] wore out. It was then taken by Qatādah ibn-al-Nu'mān who kept it until it passed on to the Caliphs. It is now in the caliphal treasury along with the Holy Relics. Its sweet scent is noticeable to anyone standing near the Holy Relics, since its grip is redolent with the perspiration of the Prophet's palm, and will diffuse therefrom like musk until the day of resurrection.

It was reported that the Prophet had three bows. One was backed (*al-mu'aqqabah*), called "The sweet smelling" (*al-rawḥā'*); another was made of the *shawḥaṭ*[2] wood, called "The white one" (*al-bayḍā'*); and the third made of the *nab'* wood, was called "The yellow one" (*al-ṣafrā'*).

When 'Uqbah ibn-'Āmir died, he left seventy bows, each with its own full quiver.

The Arab bow is that which was sent down to Adam from Paradise and which he used. It was also related that the first to construct the Arab bow and to use it was Abraham. He made a bow for each of his sons, Ishmael and Isaac, both of whom were skillful in its use. The Arab bow was also used by the Prophet Muḥammad and by his Companions. It is the same kind of bow that Gabriel carried when he appeared before the Prophet on the day of the Battle of Badr.

[1] The *siyah* was the stiff, unbending extremity of each limb of the bow. As will be observed in the later text, it was sometimes considered to be the entire end beyond the bending portion, and sometimes more strictly confined to the part up to the nock.

[2] After extended research, it is deemed probable that when the word *shawḥaṭ* is used in this connection it refers to a species of yew. *Nab'* has been defined as "white poplar," but this is by no means definitely established, and is even open to grave doubt because it is taken later in this text as synonymous with *shawḥaṭ*.

Thus it is the duty of every free, adult, and sane Moslem to learn the use of the Arab bow and teach it to his offspring.

IV. On the different kinds of bows and the most desirable of them

Bows are of two kinds: the hand bow and the foot bow. The hand bow is of three varieties: Ḥijāzi[3] Arab, composite (*maṣnū'ah*), and Persian, which is also the Turkish. The Arab bow was so called by Ishmael, the father of all the Arabs, who was the first to introduce archery among them.

The bows of the Ḥijāzi Arabs are also of three kinds. One is made of a single stave (*qaḍīb*); another is made of a stave or two staves divided lengthwise; and the third is backed, or reinforced (*mu'aqqabah*). All these three kinds are made of the *nab'*, *shawḥaṭ*, and *shiryān* wood. The method is that of shaving the wood down.[4] It is held that these three kinds of wood are in reality one, the names of which vary with the locale of growth. That which grows on the mountain top is the *nab'*, that which grows on the mountainside is the *shiryān*, and that which grows at the foot of the mountain is the *shawḥaṭ*.

[3] Ḥijāz, or Hedjaz on some maps, is that part of Arabia between the central desert and the upper half of the Red Sea. Ḥijāzi is an adjective form.

[4] This is an important sentence, as it clearly differentiates between the three kinds of Ḥijāzi bows and the true composite, for these are said to be made by reducing the size of a stave of wood by shaving down its sides, while—in the text to follow—we shall see that the composite bow is built up of substances of various origin. In fact, the author explains that the composite bow is "described as separated because of the disconnected nature of its parts before they are put together." Inasmuch as the *mu'aqqabah* (literally: reinforced) and the *murakkabah* (literally: put together) are both made of wood, horn, and sinew, this distinction in their mode of manufacture lends support to our conception of their different character as presented in footnote 6.

The bow which is made of a single stave is called *qaḍīb*; that which is made of a single stave split lengthwise is called *filq*; and that which is made of two staves split lengthwise is called *sharīj*.[5]

The reinforced bows[6] are those which have the horn of goats placed in the belly and sinew on the back. They are used only by experts or those who live near water.

The second variety of hand bow is the composite (*maṣnūʻah, murakkabah*). It is composed of four different materials: wood, horn, sinew, and glue. It has two *siyahs* [sing.: *siyah*, dual: *siyatān*], and a handle or grip (*miqbaḍ*) and is similar to the one now in use. It is called composite because of the manner of its construction. It is also described as separated, because of the disconnected nature of its parts before they are put together. Often it is called intermediate (*wāsiṭīyah*), not after the city of Wāsiṭ,[7] which it antedates, but because it occupies an intermediate position between the Ḥijāzi Arab reinforced bow and the Persian bow.

The third variety of hand bows—the Persian and Turkish—are made in the same way as the Arab composite bow.

[5] The *qaḍīb* is obviously the self bow. The *filq* seems to be a wood-backed bow, or bow with a belly of one kind of wood and an applied back of another kind, as in the case of a yew bow with the belly of heart wood and the back made of a separate piece of sap wood, glued together. In the Arabic dictionaries, the word *sharīj* is said to be sometimes synonymous with *filq*, although, in general, it appears to indicate more extensive or diverse splitting. Here, although the *filq* and *sharīj* bows are enclosed in the same category of Ḥijāzi bows, there is an implied difference. Probably the *sharīj* is a bow made of two half-*filqs* spliced at the grip, although we advance that hypothesis with diffidence because of the fact that the text gives no suggestion of transverse discontinuity. There is also a possibility, though a less likely one, that it might mean a laminated wooden bow, which is a bow of at least three layers glued together. Such bows are common in many countries, notably Japan, Belgium, France, and America, and they may be so constructed as to have many of the characteristics of the composite bow.

[6] See Appendix, 1. Reinforced Bows.

[7] Wāsiṭ means middle and the town is so called because it lies halfway down the Tigris from Baghdad to the gulf.

They have, however, long *siyahs* and short arms,[8] the *siyahs* and arms being almost, if not quite, equal to each other in size.

The central point is either in the middle of the grip or at one third of the grip from its top. Such a bow was used by both the Persians and the Turks. The Turks and most of the Persians make this bow heavy, and set it on a grooved stock (*majra*), which they fit with lock and trigger and to the end affix a stirrup, thus making it a foot bow.

Foot bows are of numerous varieties, one of which we have just described as having a lock and trigger and as being used among the Persians. Another foot bow is used by the people of Andalusia. It is, however, of no value because the Prophet has declared it accursed. This has led some learned men to maintain that all bows which are set on a stock are accursed because they resemble the cross in shape. Others maintain that such bows were condemned because they were used by the Persians, who were pagan infidels. The truth of the matter, however, is that such bows are undependable, being heavy, unwieldy, and clumsy. Upon loosing, the stock on which they are set interferes with the string and dissipates the greater part of its force.[9]

[8] The Arabic word which is translated as "arm," is *bayt*, which literally means "house." It may also denote a section of the zodiac or have usages which indicate boundaries. As "house" would not be a true translation of the sense in English, we have substituted the word "arm" because of its customary application to this part of the bow. It means the flexible portion, composed of a thin slat of wood, covered with horn on the belly and sinew on the back, which lies between the grip and the stiff, wooden *siyah*. The two arms are the sole source of power in the bow.

[9] This passage proves that the foot bow was nothing else than the crossbow in its earliest stage and, because of the new light which it sheds upon the development of projectile weapons, it is of the greatest importance. When taken in connection with the full account of the *majra* which is given in Section XLIII, we see that the channeled arrow-guide was at first held loosely in the hands for the purpose of shooting a short arrow with a long and powerful draw. When it was fastened to the bow and fitted with a lock and trigger, the crossbow was born. The name of foot bow was then applied to it because the far end was held against the ground by pressure of a foot in the stirrup while both hands were used

V. On the names and nomenclatures of the Arab bows and their different parts

We have already stated that the Arab bow is either composite or noncomposite. The noncomposite bows are those of the people of the Ḥijāz. They make them out of the *nab'*, *shiryān*, or *shawḥaṭ* wood; out of a single stave, one or two staves divided lengthwise, or a stave backed with sinew and lined with horn.

The bows may either be round, with round limbs, or flat, with flat limbs.

The composite bow is of elaborate make and careful workmanship. Its construction parallels the make-up of living things. Just as man is made of four component parts (bone, flesh, arteries, and blood) so is the bow made of four component parts. The wood in the bow corresponds to the skeleton in man, the horn to the flesh, the sinews to the arteries, and the glue to the blood. Similarly, a human being has a belly and a back, and so has a bow. And just as a man can bend inward upon his belly without any harm, but may be injured if he bends outward upon his back, so it is with a bow. It can be bent inward upon its belly but will break if it be bent upon its back.

Again, the composite bow has five sections or parts, and four joints or connecting points. The sections or parts are the two *siyahs*, the two arms, and the grip. Each section may measure one and a half spans, or one and two thirds spans, but should not go beyond that. Al-Ṭabari considered the short grip a blemish. The best opinion regarding its length is that it should be eight fingers.[10] The joints mark the meeting points of the *siyahs* with the arms and the arms with the grip.

A bow has two parts: an upper and a lower. The upper

to draw the string of the heavy bow into the lock. By experiment we have verified the fact that friction of the bowstring upon the surface of the *majra* may result in a noticeable diminution of force.

[10] See Appendix, 2. Length of the Composite Bow.

part is that which points heavenward at the time of shooting, while the lower part is that which points downward toward the earth. The limits of the upper part are the extreme end of the upper *siyah* and the width of a finger down the grip. The limits of the lower part include the rest of the bow, namely, the lower *siyah*, the lower arm, and the grip less the width of one finger which belongs to the upper part. The center of the bow would then be at a point in the grip the width of one finger from the upper arm. This is called the *kabid*, or center, and is where the arrow passes the bow at the time of shooting. As a result, the upper arm is longer than the lower and the upper *siyah* longer than the lower. This has been so designed in order to have the grip, less the width of one finger, together with the lower arm and its *siyah*, constitute one half of the bow, while the width of one finger of the grip together with the upper arm and its *siyah* constitute the other half. The arrow then passes at the middle point of the bow, which is the *kabid*. The desired balance will then obtain, and the shooting will be perfect.

The upper limb, which is also the longer of the two, is called the shooting limb (*bayt al-ramy*), and its *siyah* that of the shooting limb. It is also called the sky limb (*bayt al-ma'ani*) and the head. The shorter limb is called the dropping limb (*bayt al-isqāṭ*), and its *siyah* that of the dropping limb. It is also called the nether limb and the foot. The upper limb is called the shooting limb because it accounts for most of the shooting. It is called the head because of its upward position at the time of shooting. The lower limb is called the dropping limb because it is dropped toward the ground at the time of shooting. It is called the nether limb because it is shorter than the upper limb and because it points downward at the time of shooting. For this reason it is also called the foot.[11]

[11] Although the word *bayt* is generally used for the elastic arm, in this paragraph it refers to the whole limb and is so translated. Like *siyah*, it is capable of extended meaning.

The curved or reflexed ends of the bow are called the *siyahs*. The indentation on each *siyah* where the string is held is called the nock (*farḍ*). The part between the nock and the extremity of the *siyah* is called by the Arabs the fingernail (*al-ẓifr*), and by the professional archers the bird (*al-'uṣfūr*). The projecting part at the lower edge of each nock is called by the Arabs the cuticle (*uṭrah*), and by the professionals the string-stopper (*'aqabah*).

The part between a *siyah* and the grip is called an arm (*bayt*). The junction between an arm and its *siyah* is called the knee (*rukbah*). It is the part which bulges in and curves. What lies next to the *siyah*, toward the grip, is called the neck (*ṭā'if*, or, *'unq*). The middle part of the arm extends from the sharp point of the *siyah* to the sharp point of the grip. What lies over the *ibranjaq*, connecting it with the grip, is called by the Persians *dustār*. It is the part connected with the face of the grip from the *kabid*. The part next to the *kabid*, which is thicker and slightly higher than the grip, is called the kidney (*kulyah*). The end of each arm adjacent to the grip, where flexibility begins, is called a *daffah*. The part of the arm next to the kidney is called the spine (*abhar*). The grip is the part which the archer holds within his grasp at the time of shooting. The place where the arrow passes the bow at the time of shooting, which lies on the grip at the width of one finger from the upper arm, is the *kabid al-qaws* [literally: the middle of the bow]. The sinew which is on the back of the grip is called by the Arabs the cockscomb (*al-'urf*) and the professionals call it the horse (*al-faras*). The *ibranjaq*, according to the professionals, is a wooden piece placed on the surface of the grip on which the horns of the two arms end. The bone which covers the grip is called *khudrud*.

The bow has a back and a belly. The back is the side reinforced with sinew, and is toward your face at the time of bracing. The belly is lined with horn, and is toward your face at the time of shooting.

The Arab bows are, therefore, of four kinds: one made of a whole stave; one made of a single stave or of two staves split lengthwise; one reinforced but not composite; and one composite.[12]

VI. On the master archers

THE master archers are three: abu-Hāshim al-Māwardi [literally: The father of Hashim, the man who sells rose water], Ṭāhir al-Balkhi [Balkh is a place in northern Persia in the province of Khurasan], and Isḥāq al-Raqqi [Raqqah was a place in northern Syria]. These three men were well known for their knowledge of this profession, and their fame spread far and wide. Anyone desiring to master the art should look into their works and select for himself whatever is suitable just as al-Ṭabari did in his book *al-Wāḍiḥ* [The Clear Book].

VII. On the principles of loosing and the different schools therein

ABU-HĀSHIM AL-MĀWARDI said that the principles of shooting were four: the grasp (*qabḍah*), the clench (*qaflah*), the aim (*iʿtimād*), and the loose (*iflāt*).[13]

[12] See Appendix, 3. The Composite Bow.

[13] Because of the differences between the European and American manner of drawing with the fingers and shooting from the left side of the bow, and the Oriental manner of drawing with the thumb and shooting from the right side, we have found it necessary to coin some words, one of which is *clench*. In this translation, clench is synonymous with *lock*, the latter being perhaps a more literal translation of the Arabic word *qaflah*. In the European finger draw, the hand is wide open exposing the entire palm, but in the Oriental draw it is locked into a tight fist. The clench, or

On the other hand, Ṭāhir al-Balkhi maintained that the principles of shooting were five: the grasp, the clench, the aim, the nocking (*tafwīq*), and the loose.

Isḥāq al-Raqqi said that they were ten: standing opposite the target obliquely so that it is in line with the left eye, bracing, nocking, clenching, grasping, aiming, drawing upon the mouth, bringing the arrowhead to a stop between the two knuckles of the left thumb, loosing, and opening the hand.

Abu-Ja'far Muḥammad ibn-al-Ḥasan al-Harawi [son of Hasan who came from Herat in Afghanistan] maintained that the principles of shooting were seven: bracing, nocking, clenching, grasping, drawing, aiming, and loosing.

Some have said that the principles were four: the grasp, the draw with sixty-three [see section VIII], the aim, and the loose.

Next to the principles are the so-called branches, which comprise knowledge of nine things: of drawing evenly and steadily, of the capacity of the bow, of the capacity of the string, of the capacity of the nock of the arrow on the string, of the capacity of the arrow, of the cast of the bow, of the ability to shoot while fully armed, of accurate marksmanship, and of inflicting damage therewith.

Besides these principles and branches, an archer needs two traits: caution and patience. The principles are those without which there can be no shooting; the branches are extremely helpful.

The best school of shooting is that of Isḥāq al-Raqqi, since without standing opposite the target and aiming at it, shooting would be useless; while bracing, nocking, grasping, and loosing are indispensable and the absence of any one of them would prevent shooting. Absence of

lock, is therefore this tightly contracted arrangement of the right hand. The word *grasp*, used as a noun, which might easily be confused with *clench*, refers to the grip of the left hand on the handle of the bow. The word *grip*, however, used as a noun, we have limited to mean only the bow handle.

opening, or unclenching, the hand after loosing, however, would not prevent shooting but would gravely interfere with it.

Drawing upon the mouth and bringing the head of the drawn arrow to rest between the two knuckles of the left thumb, as well as releasing, or unclenching, the hand, are important but not indispensable. Their absence will not prevent shooting. The least important of these principles are the drawing upon the mouth and bringing the arrowhead to a stop between the two knuckles of the left thumb. On the other hand, the clenching and unclenching of the hand are very important since shooting will be greatly affected if they are not just right.

Shooting rests upon four pillars: speed, strength, accuracy, and care in self-defense. Without these four pillars the archer may perish. If he lacks speed and is slow in shooting, his adversary will destroy him before he can do anything. For this reason some archers were in the habit of making for their arrows two nocks, one crossing the other. This enabled them to insure speed in nocking and shooting.[14]

[14] This casual statement is of unusual importance as it throws additional light on one of the most controversial points in the history of archery, namely, what was meant by Roger Ascham in *Toxophilus*, which was published in 1544, when he said: "double nockinge is used for double suertye of the shafte." Nearly a page of close-set type in Elmer's *Archery* is devoted to a discussion of the meaning of that statement without reaching a definitive conclusion. It might have meant that the nock was reinforced by a longitudinal slip of horn, set in a sawn slot at right angles to the notch, as is done today and was done in an ancient English arrow found in one of the Westminster buildings. This device is for no other purpose than to prevent the shaft from breaking at the nock and might logically have been called "double nocking," though we have no specific proof that it was. That would be one kind of "suertye of the shafte." The alternate meaning might apply to the crisscross nock described here and fortunately corroborated on page 150. No English arrow with such crossed nocks is known to exist nor to have been described unmistakably in literature, though the large, bulbous ends of the ancient English arrows would give plenty of room for so much cutting. It, too, would give "suertye of the shafte" if that surety referred to quickness, and therefore safety, in fitting the arrow to the string. Now, for the first time, we have proof that two nocks did exist in one arrow.

Again, unless the archer's arrows are strong and penetrating, the adversary will divert them with his shield. Similarly, if he lacks accuracy in his marksmanship, his adversary will hold him in contempt and will easily overcome him. Finally, unless he can defend himself well, his adversary will fell him. These four things are as indispensable to the archer as are the following four to shooting: an archer, a bow, a string, and an arrow.

VIII. Things the archer should know

THERE are things which the archer should know and others which he should avoid.

An archer should learn the names of the fingers, the measured distances between their tips when outstretched, and the method of computation with them. The last is very important. Because of their ignorance of it, most writers have neglected it. Yet it is so important that it should be carefully considered and dealt with. It is based on arithmetic and reckoning.[15]

The smallest finger of the human hand is called the little finger, the next smallest is the ring finger, the third is the middle finger, the fourth is the index finger, and the fifth is the thumb.

As to the measured distances between their tips when outstretched, we first note the span (*shibr*). It is the distance between the tip of the little finger and the tip of the thumb when they are outstretched. The next is the half-

[15] It is amazing that this old manuscript on archery has vicariously resurrected the ancient Arabic system of conveying numerical values by a highly developed sign language involving the use of only a single hand. Though scholars have suspected that such a medium once existed, its details were completely lost. At present it is believed to be extinct. By its delicate and accurately formed manual postures, it is sharply differentiated from the crude gestures of ubiquitous distribution which indicate "the nine digits" and some of their more simple combinations by holding up an equal number of fingers.

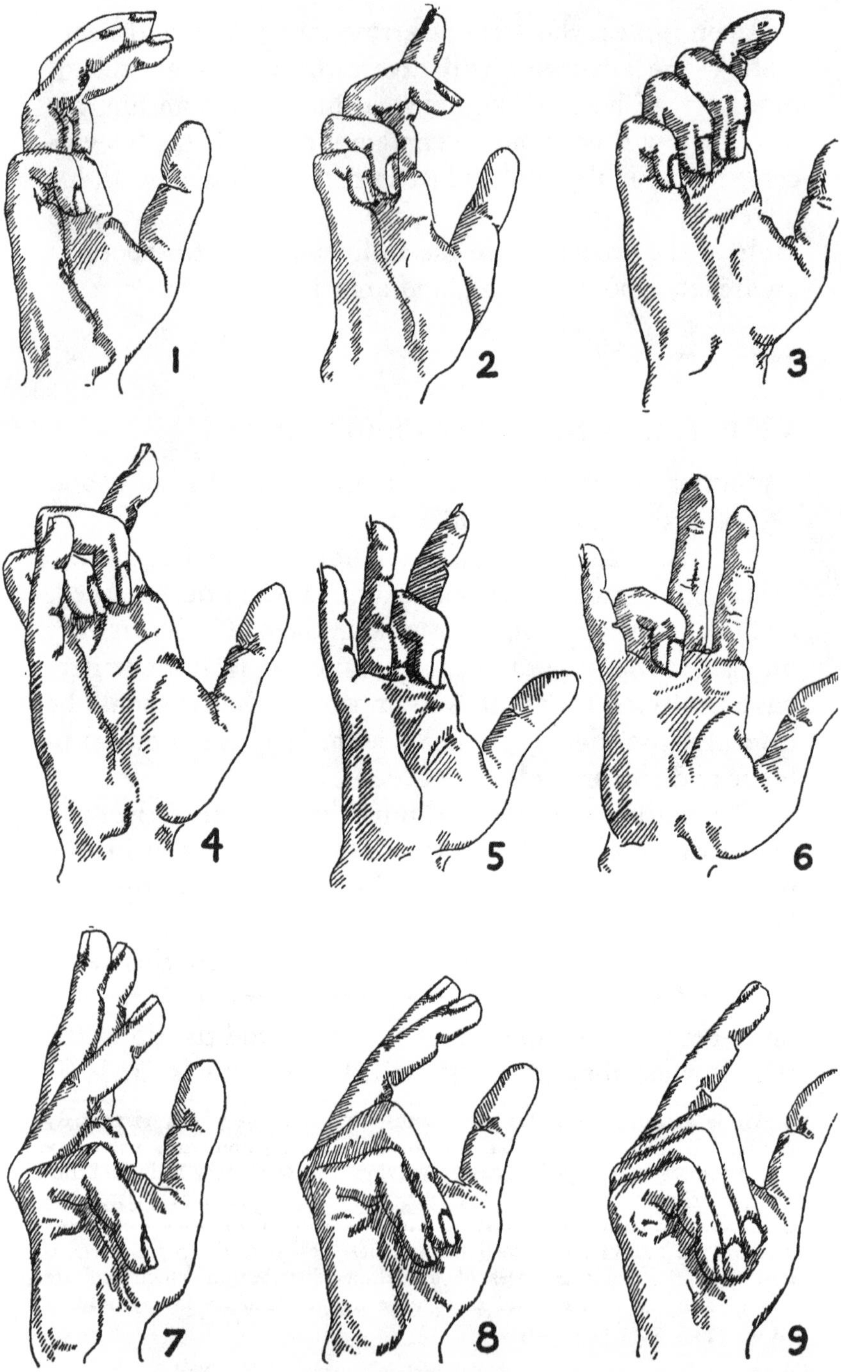

Arabic Finger Reckoning

The Digits

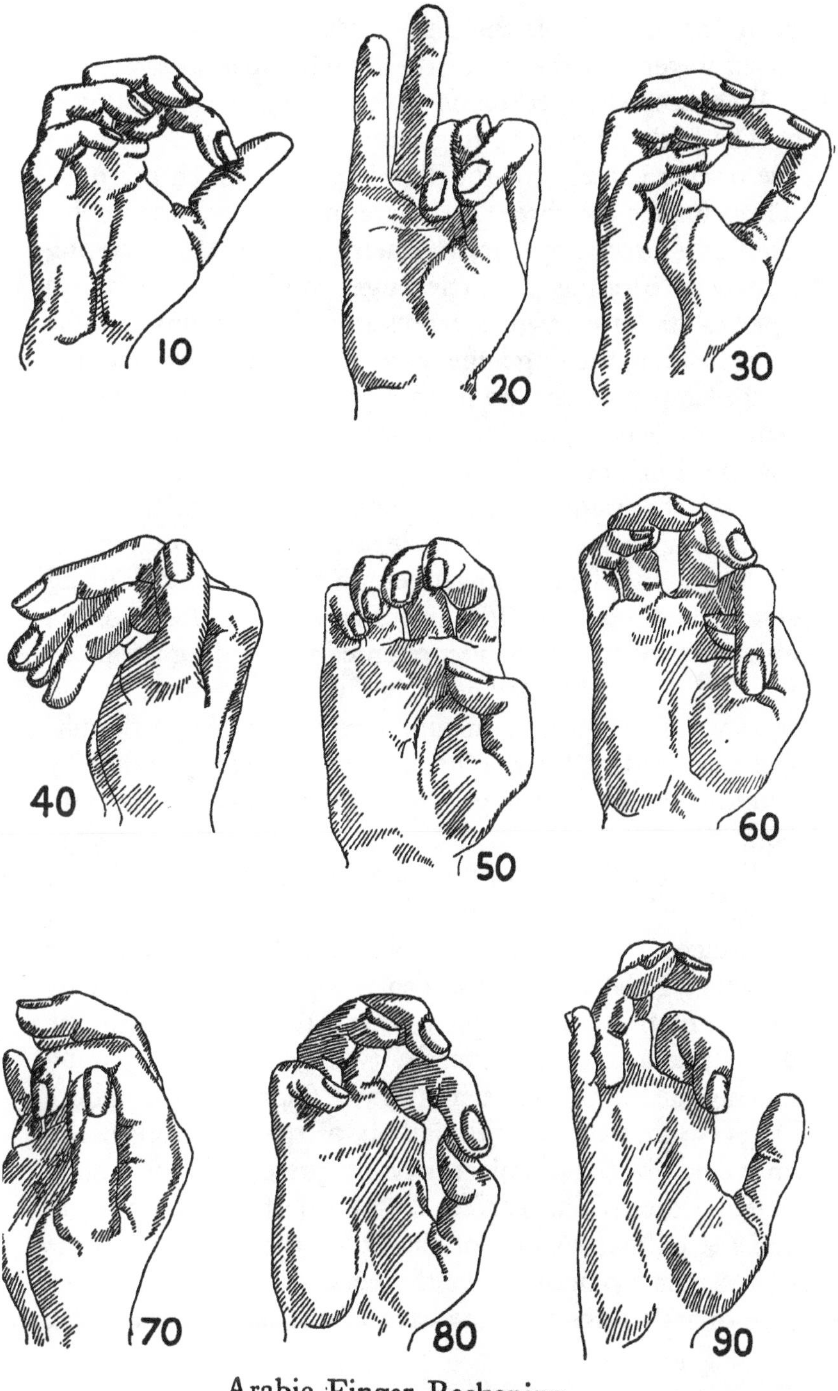

Arabic Finger Reckoning

The Tens

span (*fitr*), which is the distance between the tip of the index finger and the tip of the thumb when outstretched.

The method of reckoning with the fingers is as follows:

The little finger, the ring finger, and the middle finger are reserved solely for the digits (*āḥād*), which are nine. These fingers are three and, therefore, cannot account for the digits except by varying their position. One is represented by bending the little finger firmly, so that its tip touches its base; two is represented by bending, in the same fashion, the ring finger as well; and three by bending, in the same manner, the middle finger also. Four is represented by leaving the middle finger and the ring finger in that position and straightening out the little finger; five by leaving the middle finger alone in that position and straightening out both the little finger and the ring finger; six by leaving the ring finger bent in the same position and straightening out the little finger and the middle finger on either side of it. Seven is represented by bending the proximal joint of the little finger chiefly, so as to place the tip of that finger upon the mount at the base of the thumb; eight by bending the ring finger along with it; and nine by bending the middle finger in the same way, along with both.

The index finger and the thumb are reserved solely for the tens, which are, like the digits, nine in number. These two fingers, therefore, cannot account for the tens except by varying their positions. Ten is represented by placing the tip of the index finger on the palmar surface of the distal phalanx of the thumb; twenty is represented by placing the thumb between the index finger and the middle finger, so that the central phalanx of the index finger lies on the nail of the thumb; thirty is represented by bringing together the palmar surface of the tip of the index finger and the palmar surface of the tip of the thumb; forty is represented by twisting the thumb so that the palmar surface of its tip rests on the back of the base of the index finger; fifty is represented by bending the thumb over to the palm of the hand nearest to the base of the index finger; sixty is represented by leaving the thumb in the position it takes when representing fifty and bending over it the index finger firmly so that the latter all but surrounds it; seventy is represented by placing the tip of the nail of the thumb on the palmar surface of the middle phalanx of the index finger and turning the tip of the latter over the side of the thumb; eighty is represented by placing the tip of the index finger over the nail of the thumb; ninety is represented by bending the index finger firmly so that its tip touches its base. To represent a hundred the fingers are spread out and apart.

We shall see later how the knowledge of these various positions of the fingers is necessary in grasping the handle of the bow, drawing the string, and taking up the arrow.

The archer should also learn and practice the following four sets of things so that they may become second nature to him. These are:

Four firm: a firm grasp with his left hand; clenching with his right hand; drawing with sixty-three; the firmness of his left hand, arm, and shoulder.

Three loose: a loose index finger in his right hand; a loose index finger and thumb in his left hand; a loose arrow when the bow is drawn.

Four steady and motionless: the head, the neck, the heart, and the feet. The feet should be firmly planted on the ground.

Five straight and outstretched: the elbow, the arrowhead, the nock (*fūq*), the aim, and the posture.

The archer should also know exactly how strong is his bow and how heavy is his arrow.

To insure the utmost power in the release of the arrow four things are necessary: a firm grasp, a draw of sixty-three, a steady clench, and an even loose.

What the archer should avoid are the following fifteen

things: drawing up to his left shoulder, drawing up to his right shoulder, drawing up to his chest, drawing past his right eyebrow, drawing past his forehead, a loose grasp, slackening the clench, ignoring to open his right hand after loosing, blocking the nock of the arrow, projecting his chest, bending his left arm, holding the grip of the bow away from his wrist the width of two fingers and over by placing it in the palm of his hand, bending his head over his shoulder, opening his left hand at or before the moment of release instead of his right, and neglecting to bring the arrow to a full draw.

Archers hold that bringing the arrow to a full draw comprises half the art of archery, while the other half comprises the clench, accurate aim, and a steady left hand. It has also been said that a full draw is surely fire, while an incomplete draw is mere smoke.

THE PROPRIETIES OF ARCHERY

Among the proprieties of archery is the correct deportment in carrying the bow. When strung it should be carried in the manner in which the Apostle of God commanded that it should be carried, that is, as Gabriel carried his bow in the Battle of Badr, and as 'Ali ibn-abi-Ṭālib was wont to carry his. The Apostle of God appeared one day carrying his bow strung, his left hand grasping its grip and its string over his left arm. When the bow is not strung it should be carried with the left hand grasping the grip and the upper *siyah* pointing forward as though one were about to brace it.

Another is the manner of carrying the arrows. The arrowheads should be gathered within the right palm or interspersed between the fingers of the right hand in order to avoid hurting anyone, especially in crowded and narrow places.

Another requires the archer to bare his left arm lest the string hit his sleeve and thereby interfere with loosing.

The right arm remains covered. The Persians hold that the right arm of the archer constitutes nakedness and therefore should never be uncovered. Consequently, they have made themselves special shirts to be worn while engaged in shooting. These shirts have no sleeve for the left arm but have a long sleeve for the right arm. Upon loosing and dropping the right arm, the long sleeve likewise drops and covers it.

Another demands that the archer walk barefooted when he is picking up his arrows for shooting. This is in accordance with a tradition ascribed to the Prophet, which regards the course between the archer and his aim as a strip of Paradise.[16]

Still another requires the archer to remain erect while he shoots, whether he shoots standing or sitting; not to use too heavy a bow which is beyond his ability to control; nor to employ an arrow too long for his bow or too short. He should try his arrow before the start of any contest, for it has been said: "Fletching precedes shooting." He should also know exactly the weight of his bow, the extent of its cast, the range of its arrows, and the weight of each arrow. If the arrows are of the same weight the archer should hold them in the same way, otherwise, each according to its respective weight.

[16] Although a mystical significance is assigned to this act of walking barefooted to the target, the practical value of it is so apparent to an archer that he may wonder if such a law of religious observance did not arise as a corollary of empiricism. The compelling motive is the fear of stepping upon a snake; not on a serpent, but on a hidden arrow that is technically called a snake because it has missed the target and has buried itself so invisibly under the grass or in the sand that its presence cannot be detected by the eye. It is impossible for the layman to realize how absolute this concealment can be. An archer may hunt an hour or more for a snaked arrow—perhaps crossing and recrossing it many times—and even then may find his search to be unsuccessful; unless he finally resorts to the use of a rake or hook to scratch up the ground or should happen to tread upon the shaft and probably crunch it. To avoid this latter catastrophe the Asiatics developed the propriety of kicking off their loose shoes, so that the snake in the grass could be felt, but not broken, by their sensitive feet.

IX. How to determine the cast of the bow, its weight, and the limit of the archer's strength in drawing

THIS is one branch of archery of which the knowledge is indispensable and ignorance of it will affect shooting considerably.

The archer can determine the weight of his bow in several ways. One way is to take his bow, brace it, grasp the grip with his left hand, hold the string with the index finger, middle finger, and ring finger of his right hand, and then draw the string up to the elbow of the left arm. At this point he should release his ring finger and continue to draw until he has drawn the full length of his arrow. If he can hold the drawn bow without shaking or trembling or straining, this will be the limit of his own draw and the one fit for aiming and shooting. If, on the other hand, at the release of the ring finger, his hand should shake and tremble and be unable to draw the string to the full length of the arrow, then the bow is a heavier one than he can handle.

Another way is to take a bow, brace it, nock an appropriate arrow thereon, place its arrowhead on the ground, and, spreading the feet apart, draw the full length of the arrow. If the archer succeeds in drawing the full length of the arrow in this manner, the bow will be the right weight for him. Otherwise it is too heavy and is unfit for his use.

Having tested the bow in these two ways, the archer can then proceed to find its exact weight in pounds.[17]

After bracing the bow, he should hang it by its grip on an appropriate peg in a wall and then suspend from the middle of the string some sort of basket. Next he should

[17] Weight as applied to a bow is not its actual heft in the hand, as it is with an arrow, but is the amount of force required to draw its arrow to the head. Here "pounds" is a free translation of the Arabic measure of weight called *roṭl*, the exact value of which will be discussed in a later chapter. To convey the sense of this passage "pounds" serves very well.

nock an arrow and start filling the basket with weights until the bow is drawn to the full length of the arrow. Thereupon he should empty the basket, count his pounds, and add to them the weight of the basket itself. The result would be the weight of the bow in pounds.

HOW TO DETERMINE THE LIMIT OF AN ARCHER'S STRENGTH IN DRAWING A BOW

This method, which is called limbering, has been developed by experts and is used for practice and training. It requires a piece of wood turned to the size of the grip in thickness and length. Through one end of this a hole is bored up to about an inch from the other end. Another hole is bored horizontally from the side at a point one inch below the end which is still intact until it penetrates to the hole already bored vertically from the other end. The two holes meet at a right angle. A hook is then attached to the end which has no hole, and the piece is suspended by that hook. A stout string is passed through the end hole until it comes out through the hole in the side, whereupon a basket is attached to the string close to the ground and a loop is formed at the other end of the string. Weights equivalent to the number of pounds desired are then placed in the basket.

The archer should now place the thumb of his right hand in the loop and arrange his fingers thereon in a draw of sixty-three, in the meantime holding the piece of wood with his left hand as though he were grasping the grip of a bow. He should then draw the string in the same way as he would draw that of a braced bow. If the basket should prove too heavy he should remove some of the weights and if it should prove too light he should add thereto. In this manner an archer can determine the capacity of his draw.

Such practice is of great value to the archer who, through some reason or other, has been prevented from actual shooting with the bow. Through it he remains in trim and training. I have personally tried this operation and found it extremely useful, though rather strenuous and difficult. Attaching a pulley just above the side hole renders the drawing smoother and easier. Without the pulley I was not able to draw more than half of what I could draw with the actual bow but with it I could match that weight without any difficulty.

X. On testing the bow before bracing

NO ARCHER should ever brace a bow that is unknown to him. He should first examine it carefully and look it over very thoroughly for flaws in its construction and for injuries received from use. First he should examine the sinews on its back and test them by striking them lightly with a small piece of iron or a stone. If they resound with vibration, they are whole and fit: but if they fail to resound and seem sagging, they are loose and unfit.

He should also examine the *siyahs* for any possible flaws, such as being warped or distorted. This he does by holding the bow by its grip, with its back toward him, and carefully examining the conformity of its curves. If the bow should pass all these tests, he should not be impatient to brace. He should first hold it with its belly toward him and grasp a *siyah* with each hand. He should then place his knees against the bow on either side of the grip and gently draw the *siyahs* toward him. If the operation proceeds smoothly and both limbs bend evenly, the bow is fit and suitable.

He should then let it stand awhile before bracing it. After bracing it he should straighten out any bumps or twists that were not evident before. Then he should examine whether or not the string crosses the grip at the very center. If it does not bisect the grip he should let it go and not use it. If, however, it does so bisect the grip, he may use it, for it is straight and, by the will of God, effective.

XI. On bracing, which is the same as stringing

BRACING may be accomplished in many ways and diverse fashions. Some authors asserted that it could be done in no less than a hundred ways, while abu-Ja'far Muḥammad ibn-al-Ḥasan al-Harawi placed the number at one hundred and twenty and described them in a book which he wrote for that purpose. Most of them, however, are repetitious and useless.

There are three principles that govern bracing. The first involves moving the entire bow from one position to another, either varying the requisite acts or even ignoring some of them; the second involves omitting completely some of the important elements of bracing, with or without moving the entire bow from one position to another; the third is to move the bow to a position where it is in danger.

The first principle is to brace with one hand and one foot placed either on the back or on the neck. The second is to drop one of the things usually considered essential to bracing; namely, the placing of the *dustār* [Persian: turban], or the edge of the *dustār*, or the end of the handle, against the knee. The third is to strike the lower end of the bow against the ground and thereby brace it while one is in flight. This entails great danger of injuring the bow and should be attempted only by experts.

These principles are the nearest approximation to a generalization which covers all: nevertheless, they are not beyond objection or criticism. We shall, however, enumerate and describe in this section twelve different ways of bracing. An archer who practices these twelve methods should master their technique without feeling the need of an instructor.

The first method of bracing is called pressure bracing. It can be accomplished in two ways. The first consists of taking the string, slipping its two eyes on the bow, fastening one of the eyes into the nock of the lower limb, and pushing up the other eye the full length of the string. The point on the upper limb where the eye thus reaches is the neck (*'unq*) of the bow.

You should then hold the bow by the grip with its back toward you, spread your feet apart, and place the lower *siyah* of the bow against the base of the toes of the left foot if you happen to be barefooted, otherwise against its hollow, for it may slip off if you place it against the tip of the shoe. Then lay the upper *dustār* or, according to others, the upper end of the grip with the *dustār*, against the right knee, turn your hip firmly and smoothly, incline your head to the left lest the bow snap back and hit you, place the palm of the right hand upon the neck of the upper limb, turn the little and ring fingers of the right hand firmly and smoothly over the belly of the bow—taking care that they be not caught between the string and the *siyah*—and stretch out the thumb and index finger in order to straighten out the eye and push it into the nock. Other authorities believe that all the fingers of the right hand should be stretched out straight. Then brace the bow by pressing with your left foot against the lower *siyah* while the right palm presses against the upper neck and your left hand draws the grip toward you. With the right index finger and thumb you will finally straighten out the eye and push it into the nock.

All this should be carried out with power and firmness except that the index finger and thumb which straighten out the eye and push it into the nock should remain pliant, flexible, and free of all rigidity and strain. Throughout the entire operation all the members involved and the acts performed should be in perfect coordination, lest the bow snap or break. Once you have pushed the eye into the nock, keep your right hand pressed against the *siyah* of the upper limb, your left foot pressed against the lower *siyah*, and your left hand on the grip until you have ascertained that the bow is firm and free of any flaw; for if you release your hands before ascertaining that everything is in order, the bow may break and cause you some injury. This method of bracing has won the consensus of archers for being the best and safest for both the archer and the bow. For this reason it has been customary not to hold the archer responsible for breaking a bow if he braced it in this fashion. Rather, it was held that the bow itself must have been faulty. On the other hand, if, by any of the other methods of bracing, the bow should break, the archer was held responsible and was expected to pay an indemnity.

The second method of bracing, which is the second way of pressure bracing, is exactly like the first in every detail except that the *dustār* or, more specifically, both the end of the *dustār* and the end of the grip, is not placed against the knee. However, the first way is preferred, for the knee offers a good support.

The third method is called concealed bracing. It is suitable for the use of both the man on foot and the mounted horseman as well as for the archer who desires to conceal his bow from the enemy. It consists of placing the lower *siyah* at the root of your right or left thigh, or your right or left buttock, while your left hand holds the grip and your right hand grasps the neck of the upper limb; then, with the index finger and thumb of the right hand, straighten out the eye and push it into the nock. The bracing is completed by drawing the grip toward you with your left hand and pressing with the palm of your right hand against the neck of the upper limb. This is similar to the second alternative of the pressure bracing except for the absence of any pressure against the lower *siyah*. It is *concealed* because if the enemy were on the right of the archer, the latter would place his bow on his left and brace accordingly, or vice versa, thereby hiding his bow from the enemy.

Some divide this method into three subdivisions, according to the direction of bracing—either to the left, or to the right, or in front of the archer. The operation does not, however, differ in any of the positions. The only variation involves the position of the lower *siyah*: either at the root of the left or the right thigh, or the left or the right buttock. These variations are of no real consequence to warrant special classifications.

The fourth method of bracing is called the bracing of the frightened and fleeing archer and is among the most interesting ways of stringing a bow. If you happen to be facing an assault by sword or spear or the like, run away from your assailant placing your left hand on the grip and the palm of your right hand on the neck of the upper limb while the lower *siyah* is directly in front of you and the upper *siyah* inclined toward you. Then strike the lower *siyah* against the ground, drawing at the same time the grip toward you with your left hand and pressing with the palm of your right hand against the neck of the upper limb to the fore away from you. With the index finger and the thumb of your right hand straighten out the eye and push it into the nock. All this you do while on the run. You must be sure, however, that you strike the ground with the lower *siyah* with great care, lest you break the bow. Consequently you should not attempt this method of bracing unless you are already adept at it or have been compelled to resort to it. If you so desire, you may also grasp the bow with your left hand with its belly toward you and your right hand on the neck of the upper limb while its lower *siyah* lies between your feet. Then push the grip to the fore away from you with your left hand and draw the neck of the upper limb toward you with the right, allowing your hand to slide up the neck while the index finger and the thumb straighten out the eye and push it into the nock. The first of these two methods is quicker to perform while the second is safer for the bow.

The fifth method of bracing is called "the bracing of the wounded." It is suitable for the use of an archer who has received an injury in one of his hands, and it is among the interesting methods of bracing. It consists of inserting your foot between the string and the bow so that the string lies between your legs and the bow parallels your thigh from without. You then place its lower *siyah* in the fold of your thigh and leg and rest it against the latter, while the upper limb parallels your thigh from without. With the palm of your hand on the neck of its upper limb, you then press against the bow and allow your index finger and your thumb to straighten the eye and push it into the nock. It is indeed more appropriate to call this method "concealed bracing," because it is accomplished with one hand on one side, and is more concealed than the other. It was called "the bracing of the wounded" because an archer with a disabled arm is compelled to resort to it.

Concerning the manner in which an archer who has injured one of his arms can shoot, the following has been mentioned: The archer places the grip of the bow between the hollow of one foot and the instep of the other, lies down on his back, nocks the arrow with his uninjured hand, draws, and releases. Some archers maintain that this method of shooting is worthless; yet, in certain instances, the archer is driven to its use, particularly if one of his hands has been injured. Of course, practice in the use of this method is very helpful. Through it a degree of accuracy may be obtained. The archer should lie down on his back, raise his head and shoulders, as well as part of his back, so that the uninjured hand is raised from the ground, thereby insuring freedom of movement and avoiding hitting the ground when releasing. Furthermore, by raising his head, shoulders, and part of his back, the archer obtains a better view of his object and, therefore, a better aim.

The sixth method is called "water bracing." It is so called because of its use by archers who are standing in water which reaches up to their waists or over. It consists of placing the bow diagonally on your back, or between your shoulders, while the string rests on your face. Then hold your right hand on the neck of the upper limb, keeping the index finger and the thumb outstretched to straighten out the eye and push it into the nock. While the lower *siyah* is held firm by the left hand, you press your right forward and thereby brace the bow.

The seventh method of bracing is among the most unusual and most interesting methods. It consists of slipping the bow into your right sleeve and bringing it out through the left sleeve fully braced, quickly and without any delay. To do this you should sit down on the ground with your feet crossed, slip the lower limb in your right sleeve, hold the lower *siyah* with your left hand while the belly of the bow is up. Then place your right hand around the grip of the bow and, leaning against it, press it toward the ground firmly and strongly, sliding the back of the upper limb and its *siyah* against your right thigh. The eye would then be pushed into the nock by your thigh. You then bring it out through your left sleeve fully braced. The whole operation should be performed without pause or interruption. At first it is better to practice this method outside your sleeve and then, after it has been perfected outside, do it inside.

The eighth method of bracing is called "the bracing of the archers." It consists of sitting down on the ground with crossed legs, releasing the eye of the string from the upper limb completely, and placing it in the hand of someone who will later insert it into the nock. Hold the bow with the left hand on the back of the *siyah* of the lower limb and the right hand on the back of the *siyah* of the upper limb, as close as possible to the nock. Then place your knees against the limbs of the bow—the belly being toward you—and with both hands draw the *siyahs* toward you with gentleness and care until the bow is in the position of bracing; whereupon the person who holds the eye of the string will insert it into the nock. This method of bracing is especially desirable when the archer is bracing an unfamiliar bow, because he draws it gently and carefully.

The ninth method of bracing is called both "the bracing of the archers" and "the bracing of the lone archer," because the archer himself inserts the eye of the string into the nock without the aid of an assistant. It is accomplished by sitting down on the ground with crossed legs, freeing the upper eye clear of the bow, holding the back of the lower *siyah* close to the nock with the right hand and the back of the upper *siyah* close to the nock with the left, while the belly is toward you; then—raising the left knee a little and placing it against the belly of the bow—drawing the *siyahs* gently toward you until the bow reaches the position of bracing. Thereupon, you place the lower *siyah*, which you have been holding with your right hand, on your right knee, while the upper *siyah* lies at the top of your left knee, and finish by taking the eye with your right hand and inserting it into the nock.

The whole operation can be performed in reverse by holding the lower *siyah* with the left hand and the upper *siyah* with the right hand, raising the right knee and placing it against the belly of the bow, drawing the *siyah* gently toward you, and inserting the eye with the left hand. For this reason—namely, the possibility of carrying out these two methods in reverse—the two bracings of the archers have been regarded as constituting four methods.

The tenth method of bracing consists in releasing the eye from the nock of the upper *siyah*, placing the lower *siyah* against the base of your right or left thigh while the bow lies along your side and back and up past your neck, and then holding the upper *siyah* with one hand and drawing gently until it reaches the position of bracing. Thereupon, you insert the eye in the nock with your right hand if you had the lower *siyah* at the base of the right thigh, or with your left hand if you had it at the base of your left thigh. This has also been considered to constitute two methods of bracing.

The eleventh method of bracing is performed by freeing the upper eye of the string clear of the bow, stretching the right leg and bending the left to a kneeling posture—or, if you wish, you may reverse the operation by extending the left and bending the right—and then, with the belly of the bow toward you, placing a hand on the back of each *siyah* close to the nock, press against the grip of the bow with either the right or left foot, depending on which was the one outstretched. You then draw the *siyahs* gently toward you, while the foot makes counterpressure on the grip, until the bow reaches the position of bracing. Thereupon, you place one *siyah* against your bent knee, after you have raised it a little from the ground, and insert the eye into the nock with the hand that is thus freed. This has also been regarded as constituting two methods of bracing.

The twelfth method of bracing is used in the case of very strong bows where the preceding methods are of no avail. It consists of grasping the grip with both hands while the back of the bow is toward you, placing your left foot against the back of its lower *siyah* and your right foot against the back of the neck of its upper limb next to the eye of the string; then, simultaneously drawing the grip with both hands and pushing with your feet, the left foot remains against the back of the lower *siyah* while the right foot slides with the eye along the neck of the upper limb toward the nock until the eye settles therein.

The principles involved in all the methods of bracing

are four: putting the lower *siyah* of the bow in a place where it will be held firmly, like the hollow of the foot or the base of the thigh; grasping the grip with the left hand; pressing the palm of the right hand against the neck of the upper limb; and, with the index finger and thumb of the right hand, straightening out the eye and pushing it into the nock.[18]

XII. On the curvature of the bow after bracing

If one of the two limbs of the bow is slightly stronger than the other and yet you desire to have both curve equally, you had better use "the bracing of the lonely archer," which is the ninth method of bracing that is described in the preceding section. Place a knee against the weaker limb while bracing and, as a result, the bow will be straight and of proper curvature. Or you may use "the pressure bracing," which is the first method described in the preceding section. Place the *siyah* of the weaker limb against the base of your toes while the palm of your right hand presses against the neck of the stronger limb, and the bow will be straight and of proper curvature after it is braced. If, however, the disparity between the two limbs is great, it cannot be rectified unless you use a file or resort to fire.

XIII. On unstringing

Numerous methods of unstringing the braced bow have been described. Most of these, like the methods of bracing, are repetitious and useless. We shall, however, describe six methods which we deem sane or reasonably sane, and shall reject the rest as being unsound.

[18] See Appendix, 4. Bracing.

The first and basic method, which underlies all other methods and is used by beginners and experts and by those who shoot while sitting down, consists of raising both knees and spreading them apart, placing them each against one of the two limbs of the bow, the belly of which is toward you, and holding with each hand the tips of the two *siyahs* while the index finger of your right hand is outstretched along the length of the upper *siyah* by the eye of the string. You then draw the *siyahs* toward you gently and slowly until the string becomes loose; thereupon you push the eye of the string out of the nock with your outstretched index finger. You will then release the pressure gently and gradually until the unstrung bow takes its normal shape. No one who breaks a bow while unstringing it in this fashion is held responsible for the damage though he who breaks it while unstringing it by any other method is held responsible therefor and is required to pay damages.

The second method of unstringing, also used by one who shoots while sitting down, consists in placing the lower *siyah* on your left thigh, while your left hand holds the grip and your right holds the back of the upper *siyah*; the index finger of your right hand is outstretched along the length of the upper *siyah* next to the eye of the string and the belly of the bow is facing toward you. You then, with your right hand, draw the upper *siyah* up while your left presses against the grip downward. When the string is thus loosened, the index finger of your right hand plucks the eye out of the nock. Then you release the pressure of your left hand off the grip gradually and slowly and your right hand removes its upward pressure off the upper *siyah* until the bow regains its normal unstrung length.

The third method, suitable for the person who shoots while standing, consists in raising your left knee and placing the lower *siyah* against it while your left hand holds the grip and the fingers of your right hand press against the back of the upper *siyah*, which you draw upward; simultaneously, your left hand presses downward. As the string becomes loose, you push its eye out of the nock with your index finger. You then release your hands gradually until the bow reaches its outstretched limit.

The fourth method of unstringing, used by horsemen, consists of placing the lower *siyah* against the neck of the horse, or against your own thigh, and continuing the operation described in the preceding method.

The fifth method of unstringing consists in placing the lower *siyah* on the ground with your left hand holding the grip and your right against the back of the upper *siyah* while the index finger of your right hand is outstretched in order to push the eye out of the nock. You then continue the operation described in the third method of bracing.

The underlying principles of unstringing are four: placing the lower *siyah* in some place where it will be held firm, holding the grip with your left hand, pressing against the back of the upper *siyah* with your right, and pushing the eye of the string out of the nock with the outstretched index finger of the right hand. The belly of the bow is, throughout, toward you.

The sixth method of unstringing consists in holding the *siyahs* of the bow with your hands close to the nocks while the index finger of your right hand is outstretched along the length of the *siyah* in order to push therewith the eye of the string out of the nock. One of your feet presses against the grip. You then draw the *siyahs* toward you, push the grip with your foot away from you, and complete the operation as described before.

XIV. On picking up the bow and arrow preparatory to shooting and the manner of shooting

A BOW is either strung or unstrung. If it is strung and lying on the ground, you should seize the grip with your left hand, placing the string along the back of your left arm and the belly of the bow toward you. You should then pick the arrow up gently with the thumb, index finger, and middle finger of your right hand, just as a scribe takes a pen, while the small and ring fingers remain folded against the palm. This is the manner advocated by the school of abu-Hāshim. You may also pick the arrow up with the five fingers of the right hand, just as the horseman picks up a spear. This is the fashion advocated by the school of Ṭāhir al-Balkhi. Or, if you so desire, you may pick it up with the index finger and the middle finger at a point one span away from its arrowhead; just as a bird picks up a piece of straw with its beak for the building of its nest. This is the method preferred by the school of Isḥāq al-Raqqi.

Then you revolve the grip in your palm—thereby transferring the string to a position along the front part of the arm—and release the thumb, index, and middle fingers off the grip so that it is held by the small and ring fingers. This is the method advocated by the schools of abu-Hāshim and Isḥāq. You then bring the right hand with the arrow near to the left that holds the grip and place the shaft of the arrow between the thumb, index finger, and middle finger of the left hand at a point the measure of a fist from its head. This is the method followed by the school of Isḥāq.

You may also leave your three fingers grasping the grip without releasing them therefrom. When you bring your hands near to each other at the grip you may open the same three fingers in a way which resembles the opening of the blades of shears. The bringing of both hands together and the opening of the fingers should be done simultaneously.

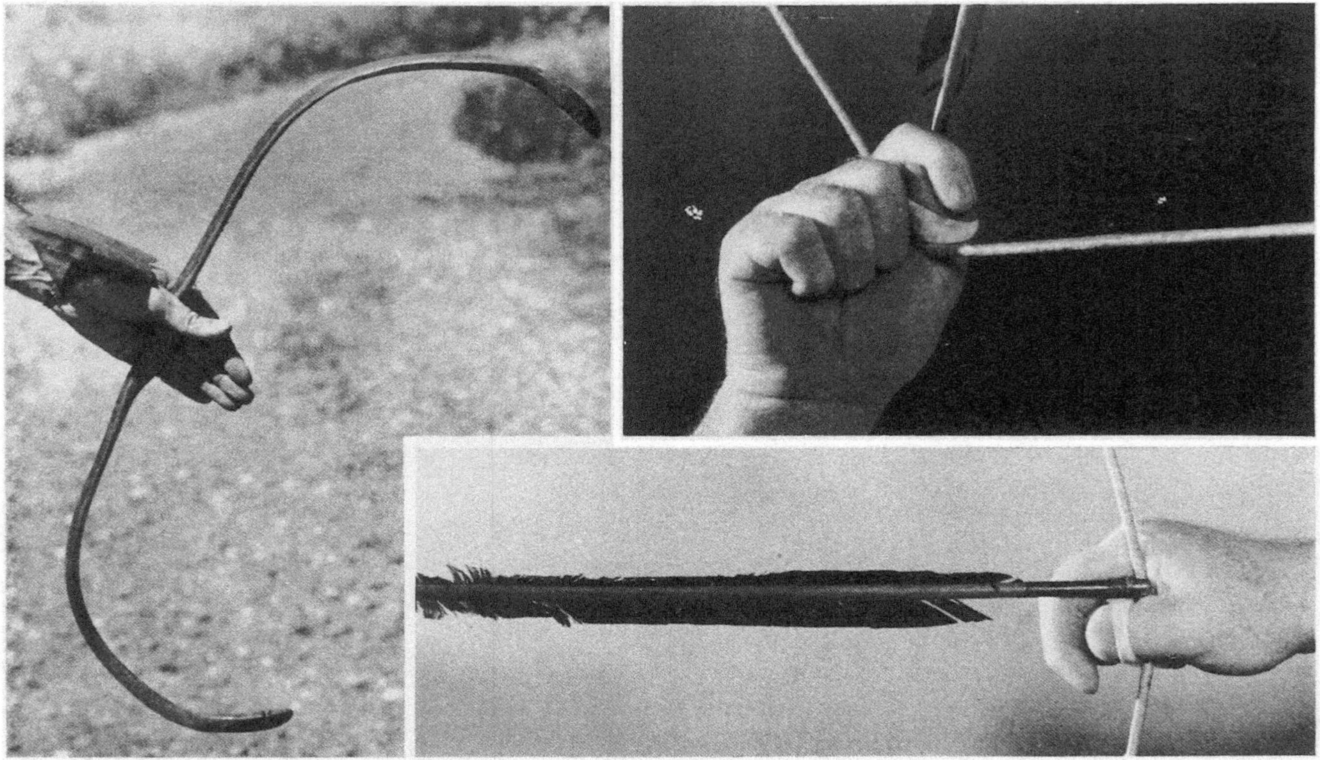

Left. Turkish Bow and Siper. *Above, right*. Demonstrating the Lock Called "Sixty-three," Showing the Fingers and the Engagement of the String on the Ring. *Below, right*. Demonstrating the Lock Called "Sixty-three," Using a Real Turkish Thumb Ring and a Chinese Bow and Arrow

You then place the arrow between the three open fingers at a point one span from its head, locking them thereon with thirty-eight, and run the other hand on the remaining part of the stele. This is the method of the school of Ṭāhir.

This running of the hand along the stele is done to insure freedom from shavings or strewn feathers and the like. When you have run your hand on the stele down to the nock, hold your index finger and thumb very firmly on either side of the nock, with the slot resting against the first phalanx of your middle finger close to the finger tip. This is the method advised by the school of abu-Hāshim. You may also hold to either side of the nock with the middle phalanx of your index finger, the fore part of the thumb, and the tip of the middle finger. This is the method of the school of Ṭāhir. Or, you may hold the nock with the index finger and the thumb, placing the slot of the nock between the first two phalanges of the middle finger. This is the method of the school of Isḥāq.

You then give the arrow a hard and quick shove while the stele is against the string until it is clear past the string, which will hit the base of your thumb and index finger. Thereupon, you will bring the arrow back to the string and nock it. This is the method of abu-Hāshim. You may also give the arrow a hard and quick shove while the stele is against the string without going clear past the string, but, as soon as the nock reaches the string, you open your fingers and nock it. This is the method of Ṭāhir and Isḥāq. Ṭāhir used to hear a sound from the bow and arrow at the time of nocking.[19]

[19] There is really very little to choose between these two schools of nocking, the difference being only in the slight difference in space lying between the string and arrow before the nocking is completed. We have always practiced and taught the method of Ṭāhir and Isḥāq, but among Americans in general it is rarely used. Nearly all Americans nock an arrow by holding it above the feathers and placing it on the string like a woman sticking a clothespin on a washline.

Since all sounds originate in vibration, the one which Ṭāhir heard was due to the peculiar shape of the Oriental nock. Its slot is wide and

Throughout the operation you should not watch the nocking nor any of the details that lead to it. Rather keep your eyes upon the target. This is the method of all three schools. Furthermore, the whole operation should be carried out before you, opposite your chest, or, according to others, opposite your navel.

If, on the other hand, the bow were unstrung while lying on the ground, then you should hold it in the manner we have already described under bracing, brace it, and continue the operation described above in the first method.

There are some who, while standing, would hold the tip of the upper *siyah* with the left hand, place the lower *siyah* on the ground as though it were a cane, and then bend over, pick the arrow up and revolve it between the index finger and the middle finger of the right hand, and toss the bow gracefully upward into the left hand (all these operations taking place simultaneously), catch it at the grip by the same left hand with which the bow was tossed upward, strike the arrow against the inner part of the grip (others strike it first against the inner part and then against the outer part), all after revolving the arrow between the two fingers, and then continue the operation described under the first method, such as bringing the hands together by the grip, and so on, until the arrow is nocked.

rounded, to give freedom to the string, but it has narrow lips to keep the arrow from falling off. Thus the narrow opening would pluck the string and the wide nock would give it room to vibrate. The whole would be instantaneous and would indicate a strong bow and perfectly fitted arrow and string such as one might expect from a master archer.

XV. On the different draws and the manner of locking the thumb and the index finger on the string, and on the rules of arranging the index finger upon the thumb

THE draws agreed upon by experts are six: the sixty-three, sixty-nine, seventy-three, eighty-three, twenty-four, which is called the *Khusruwāni* [after Chosroës, king of Persia], and seventy-two, which is called the reserve. Whatever draws there are besides these are of little use. The strongest and most useful of these draws is the sixty-three, followed by the sixty-nine, which, though weaker, is supposed to be smoother and more accurate. It is weaker because it lacks the clench. Most archers use these two draws.

The seventy-three is weaker and easier to draw, but it is faster in release. The eighty-three is supposed to be stronger and therefore can be used with heavier bows, though it is very much like the seventy-three in release. The reserve draw, which is the seventy-two, is the draw of the non-Arabs. It is good for drawing strong bows and for practicing with them. It is, however, difficult to release. It consists of locking the index finger and the middle finger upon the thumb.[20]

The twenty-four draw is worthless except in drawing supple bows employed in trick shots. It was current among the Turks and Greeks because they employed nondescript and supple bows and locked their fingers in whatever draw occurred to them. They also had the twenty-one draw which, in weakness, is like the twenty-four. The exact manner of these draws may be learned from the section on finger reckoning and computation already described (Section VIII).

The Slavs (al-Ṣaqālibah) have a peculiar draw which

[20] While this description is clear, the lock is certainly not "seventy-two" as described earlier.

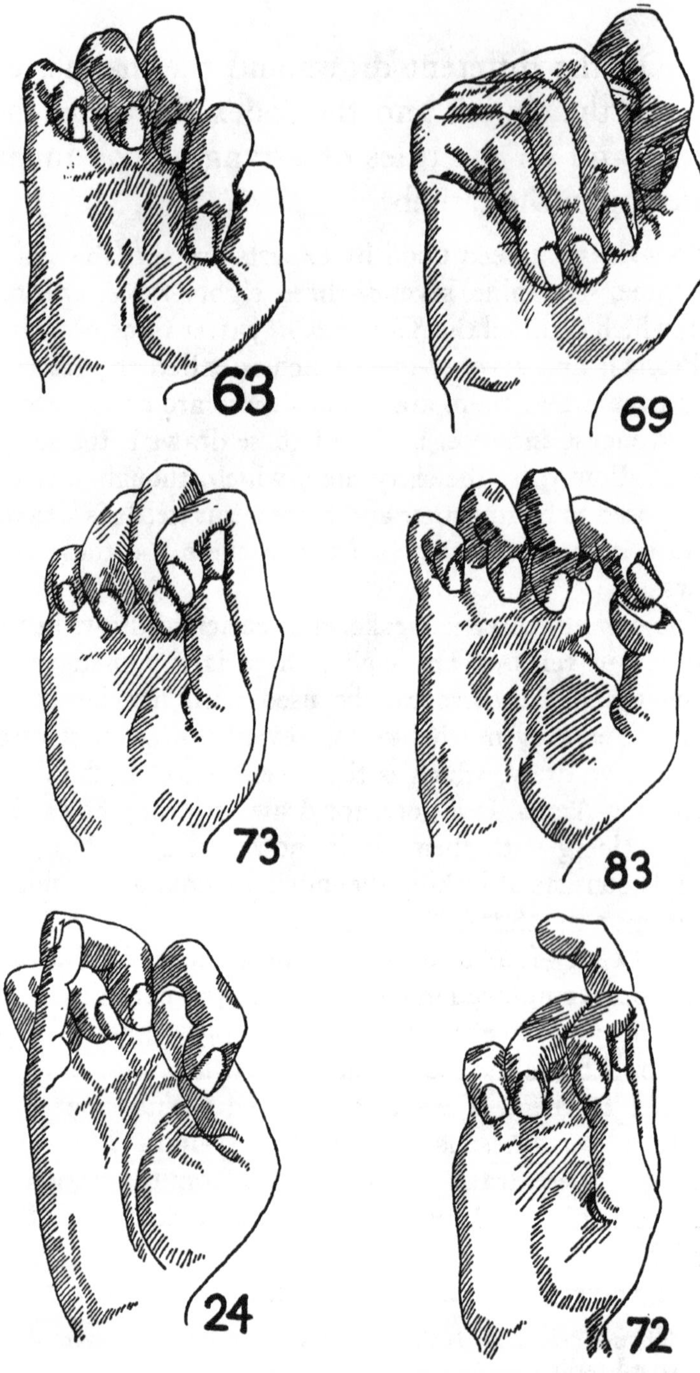

The Six Different Draws or "Locks" According to the Arabic System of Finger Reckoning

consists of locking the little finger, the ring finger, and the middle finger on the string, holding the index finger outstretched along the arrow, and completely ignoring the thumb. They also make for their fingers finger tips of gold, silver, copper, and iron, and draw with the bow upright.

The Greeks have a draw which consists of locking the four fingers—the index finger, the middle finger, the ring finger, and the little finger—while the bow is in a horizontal position (*rāqidah*); and, holding the arrow between the middle finger and the ring finger, drawing toward the chest. This is indeed a corrupt draw used by the ignorant.

Regarding the exact manner of the draw, experts have disagreed as to where the string should be in relation to the thumb as well as where the tip of the thumb and the index finger should be. Some hold that the string should rest in the middle of the distal phalanx of the thumb obliquely toward the tip, while the tip of the thumb lies upon the top of the middle phalanx of the middle finger, and the middle phalanx of the index finger lies upon the middle of the distal phalanx of the thumb with the distal phalanx of the index finger bent over the side of the thumb, and the joint of the base of the index finger next to the knuckle of the thumb beside the nock. In drawing you widen the space between the thumb and the middle finger while the tip of the index finger lies outside the string [to the left]. This is the method of abu-Hāshim al-Māwardi. Al-Ṭabari related that al-Māwardi was wont to place the tip of his index finger inside the string [to the right]. This, I believe, is an error by the scribe, otherwise, a mistake resulting from his ignorance, because placing the string obliquely in the joint of the thumb, which is the method of abu-Hāshim, precludes the possibility of holding the tip of the index finger inside the string.

Others hold that the string should be in the joint of the thumb straight without any obliqueness, while the tip of the thumb lies upon the top of the middle phalanx of the middle finger, from which the thumb will not be separated in drawing, and the inner part of the phalanx next to the nail of the index finger upon the nail of the thumb just below its knuckle and down to a third of its nail. The tip of the index finger should be inside the string. This is the method of Ṭāhir as reported by al-Ṭabari under the section on clenching on the string.

Still others hold that the string should rest just in front of the joint of the thumb, close to it, while the index finger is inside the string. This is the method of Isḥāq. Some of the authors on this science related that the method of the experts was to place the tip of the index finger on the string, for it insures greater accuracy and strength and quicker release. Consequently there are three schools concerning the position of the tip of the index finger: to hold it outside the string, inside the string, and on the string. The first draw, with the oblique position of the string in the joint of the thumb, insures the quickest release, and is the oldest method. It was used by the expert Persian archers. The second, with the straight position of the string in the joint of the thumb, offers the strongest draw. The third gives a quicker release than the second and a greater range than either. It is used by the experts of our day.

XVI. On how to hold the grip of the bow with the left hand

EXPERT archers have disagreed on the exact manner of holding the grip of the bow with the left hand. Abu-Hāshim was wont to hold the grip with acute obliqueness, placing it between the groove formed by the proximal joints of the four fingers of his left hand and that formed by the middle joints of the same, while the upper end of the grip touched the base of his left thumb close to the proximal phalanx, and the lower end lay at a point the width of one and a half to two fingers away from his wrist. He then pressed the hypothenar eminence against the grip, tightening the little finger as hard as possible, the ring finger a little less, the middle finger a little less than the ring finger, and the index finger still a little less than the middle finger, while the thumb remained loose either in front of the grip or behind it. This method was followed by the Persians, particularly by archers like Shāpūr dhu-'l-Aktāf, Bahrām Gur [both of whom were kings of Persia], and others besides.

Ṭāhir used to hold the grip with his entire palm, pressing against it with both the thenar and hypothenar eminences. In fact, he was wont to place the grip in the joint at the base of the four fingers of his left hand and grasp it gently with his five fingers after pushing the flesh at the base of his fingers toward the center of his palm, resting the upper end of the grip between the two phalanges of his thumb, and the lower end in the groove between the two eminences. He would then tighten his grasp until his finger tips all but bled, and press hard with his wrist against the grip.

Isḥāq was in the habit of striking a happy medium between the two methods. He placed the grip in the joint of the second phalanges of his left hand while laying its upper end against the proximal phalanx of his thumb and its lower in the palm a finger's breadth from the wrist bone. Then he tightened the three fingers—middle, ring, and little—of the left hand very hard but allowed the index finger to remain loose either in front of the grip or behind it. The arrangement of the fingers would then be a thirty, which is the best method of holding the grip.

An archer who follows the method of holding the grip straight should tighten all his fingers except the thumb, as we have already described, and should press against it with the whole base of his hand. This method is best for shooting at near targets, making trick shots, and for practicing with a very strong bow. He who uses this method, however, cannot avoid having the string hit against his forearm. This militates against the utility of the method.

An archer who holds the grip obliquely should tighten his fingers in the order which we have already described and should press against it with the hypothenar eminence. This method is best for shooting at high objects, such as walls or fortifications. It is also stronger than the former, though less accurate.

An archer who follows the middle course will neither hold the grip with his entire hand nor hold it therein obliquely. It is, as we have already stated, the best method.

Summing up, the method of holding the grip straight is that of the Arabs, while that of holding it obliquely is that of the Persians. The basis of the difference is their disagreement concerning facing the target. Those who face the target sideways should make the grip of the bow square and should hold it obliquely. To hold it straight is wrong and will spoil the accuracy of shooting. Those who choose to face the target halfway between the sideway position and the frontal position should make the grip neither square nor round but halfway between. Furthermore, the size of the grip should be proportional to the size of the archer's hand, so that he may hold it with ease and comfort. The best size in proportion to the hand is that which leaves, after grasping with the whole hand, a space between the finger tips and the palm equal to the width of half a finger. If the grip is too small, the defect can be remedied by wrapping around it firmly a piece of rag or tape.

Archers throughout the world have agreed that strong and accurate shooting depends upon a firm hold upon the grip so that the finger tips all but bleed. The Persians, however, maintained that the opposite, namely, a loose hold upon the grip, insured strength and accuracy. This, to my mind, is wrong.

XVII. On the clench

THE clench is considered by all archers as one of the basic principles of archery. It consists in folding the little finger, the ring finger, and the middle finger tightly to the palm of the right hand, forming thereby a hollow duct, and concealing the nails completely. This is the method of Ṭāhir. Or you may fold them tightly without forming a hollow, though the first method is superior. It is said of abu-Hāshim that no one could ever see the little finger or ring finger when he was shooting, either from his right or from his left.

XVIII. On drawing and its limits

ARCHERS have disagreed concerning drawing. Some have maintained that an archer should draw the length of the arrow less the width of a fist and pause for a count of one or two, or, according to some, a count of three. He should then draw the remaining length of the arrow with a sudden jerk and release. Others draw steadily the whole limit of the arrow to its very end and release without any pause or holding. Among the followers of this second method some pause for a count of two while others pause for a count ranging between two and ten. These are the followers of the intermediate school.

Its limits are fifteen in number: five are connected with the left hand of the archer, five with his right hand and body, and five with his face. The five connected with his left hand are: first, bringing the arrowhead to the tip of the nail of his thumb; second, bringing the tip of the arrowhead to the base of his thumb; third, bringing the tip of the arrowhead to the first knuckle of his thumb; fourth, bringing the tip of the arrowhead halfway between the two knuckles of his thumb (this is called the full draw); fifth, bringing the tip of the arrowhead to the lower knuckle of his thumb. Only the first is good for warfare, while the second, third, and fourth are good for target shooting. The fifth is risky and poor, its use lacking any advantage.

The five connected with the right hand and the body are: first, drawing until the forearm meets the upper arm and both are held closely to each other; this is called the bleeder's hold;[21] second, drawing to the shoulder joint and dropping the hand along the fore part of the shoulder just removed from the joint, or, according to others, just on the joint, and pausing for a count ranging between two and ten; third, drawing to the back of the ear between the shoulder joint and the lobe of the ear; fourth, drawing to the throat; fifth, drawing to the base of the breast.

The first, or bleeder's hold, is the best because it involves no effort or artificiality. The second and third involve a great deal of effort and artificiality as well as weakness, because the arrow is released by the action of the bow rather than by that of the hand, since the hand is left no freedom for movement, traction, or pull. The fourth and the fifth, which are drawing to the throat and to the base of the breast, are worthless because it is not possible to aim accurately with them. Others, however, have said that they are good for long distances; consequently their arrows are long.

The five connected with the face are: first, drawing to

[21] Bleeding from minor wounds on the flexor surface of the forearm is lessened or even checked by thus squeezing together the two parts of the arm.

the extreme end of the right eyebrow; second, drawing to the lobe of the ear; third, drawing to the white spot where no hair grows between the lobe of the ear and the beard; fourth, drawing to the end of the right jawbone, in which operation the arrow runs along the lips or the mustaches; fifth, drawing to the chin.

The first, namely, drawing to the extreme end of the right eyebrow, is decidedly wrong and is practiced by those who are ignorant of the principles of archery, since it is blind. Furthermore, the right hand is thereby at a higher level than the left and, therefore, the arrow travels downward to the earth. For this reason some have recommended the method for shooting from on high, as from fortresses and similar elevated places. It is, however, useless for target shooting because it is blind. It has been said that the arrows used therein are long and offer, as a result, strength in drawing. It is an ancient way of shooting and, on the authority of al-Ṭabari, the method of the intermediate school.

Drawing to the lobe of the ear is, likewise, an ancient method of shooting and is very accurate. There is not among the ancient methods any which is more accurate or more deadly. Drawing to the white spot between the lobe of the ear and the side of the beard is almost as good as drawing to the lobe of the ear; whereas drawing to the end of the right jawbone and running the arrow along the lips or the mustaches is the method used by the advocates of the straight and level position of the arrow and was the practice of the people of Khurasan as well as that of Ṭāhir al-Balkhi, Isḥāq al-Raqqi, and others besides. It is the best method. This straight and level position of the arrow calls for a perfectly horizontal state where the arrowhead is level with the nock of the arrow, free of any inclination either upward or downward. It is indeed the best method for target shooting and no other method is more accurate or deadly because it is the least subject to errors and the most consistent in hitting the mark. It is the favorite method of experts.

Drawing to the chin where the mustache and the beard meet at the root of the lower teeth is faulty because it, too, is blind, removed from the sight. It is, therefore, not unlike drawing to the throat and the root of the breast.

This paragraph treats of the basic rule governing the length of the arrow. An archer desiring to determine the length of his arrow should pick up a bow, string it, and, taking an arrow, nock and draw it to one of the limits connected with his left hand, while bringing his right hand to one of the limits connected with his face and with his body and right hand—in every case the limit best suited and most comfortable to him. He should cut the arrow off at the point marking the limit of his draw. This would then be his most suitable arrow; he should not use another. This is what I myself worked out from the various methods of the other experts and developed from their principles.

XIX. On aiming, which is the same as pointing at the target

Aiming is the highest as well as the greatest, most difficult, and most abstruse principle of archery. It is the basis of all shooting. Experts have disagreed concerning it and have divided into three schools.

The first school looks at the target from the outside of the bow, the second from the inside of the bow, and the third from both the outside and the inside of the bow.

The inside of the bow is the side toward your right and along which the arrow passes at the time of release; the outside is the other side which is toward your left. This should be carefully remembered because it is of basic importance in this section.

The method of the first school, namely, looking at the target from outside the bow, has three variations. The first consists of aligning the arrowhead with the target and focusing the sight on both with both eyes from outside the bow and, finally, aiming with the left eye. When the arrowhead disappears from sight, the archer frees the arrow immediately with a quick release.

The second variation consists of aligning the arrowhead with the target, focusing the sight on both with the left eye from the outside of the bow and aiming therewith, while at the same time the right eye is focused on the *dustār* of the bow, completely blind to the target, the head is straightened, and the lower *siyah* is brought a little to the left side. This is the method of abu-Hāshim al-Māwardi.

The third variation consists of focusing the sight of both eyes on one point by bringing the pupil of the left eye to its exterior angle and that of the right eye to its interior angle. This type of aiming is called the squinting aim and by some is supposed to be the best of the three. In the opinion of the author, however, it is the worst and most faulty and possesses the greatest margin of error; for if the archer should close one eye and open the other and aim with it by sighting obliquely,[22] and then should close the eye which he had left open and open the one which was closed and should aim with it, he would realize that the aim of the two eyes in this position is never the same. How then could aim taken by this method be accurate?

In my judgment the best of the three kinds of aiming is that of abu-Hāshim.

These three variations which involve looking toward the target from the outside of the bow are all suitable for

[22] We interpret this word—oblique, obliquely—with reference to the turn to the left of the head on the neck. Actually, the position of the archer is sidewise to the target but, because of anatomical limitation, the head cannot be turned fully to the left—at least in most archers—and, therefore, must remain at an angle, or oblique, to the direction of the arrow, or line of aim.

archers who face the target while seated or who stand obliquely as well as for those who are mounted or are in full armor. They are very effective because of the length of the draw that is used in them. They comprise the ancient method of aiming which was in universal use among the kings of Persia and expert archers.

The second school, namely, that of sighting at the target from the inside of the bow, has two variations. The first consists of aligning the arrowhead upon the target, focusing the sight upon both by both eyes, and maintaining it thereon throughout the operation of drawing. When the arrowhead reaches the thumb, the arrow is released.

The other variation of the second school consists in focusing the sight upon the arrowhead and the target with the right eye while drawing the arrow, and aiming therewith while the left eye is focused upon the *dustār* of the bow. On seeing the arrowhead reach the thumb, the arrow is released. This method is very accurate, and is suitable for shooting at near and small targets as well as for trick shooting. It is, however, extremely difficult as well as weak and ineffective, because the archer—seated as he is with crossed legs and facing the target directly—is unable to prolong his draw; consequently, the force of the arrow is weakened. There is no room in it for the least sudden jerk or pull before the release.

The third school, namely, looking at the target from both the outside and the inside of the bow, also has two variations. The first consists of holding the bow so that the upper end of the grip is on a level with the nose, aligning the arrowhead with the target, focusing the sight on both with the left eye from the outside of the bow and with the right from the inside, and drawing horizontally on a level with the lips up to a point the width of a fist from the arrowhead, at which point the draw is completed with a sudden jerk or pull and the release is made.

The second variation consists of aligning the arrowhead

with the target and focusing the sight upon both with both eyes from outside the bow. After drawing two thirds of the arrow length until the arrowhead can be seen no longer, the left eye is kept in focus upon the target while the right eye watches the movement of the arrow from the inside of the bow. When the arrowhead reaches the thumb, the arrow is released.

Some writers on the subject have asserted that this second variation of the third school is the best one, being more accurate and less subject to error than any other method. The archer using it looks at the target from a position halfway between the frontal view and the oblique side view, thereby avoiding the shortcomings of both and being enabled to insure an accurate aim.

According to the testimony of al-Ṭabari, the first variation is the method of Isḥāq al-Raqqi, while the second is not far removed from it.

A person desiring to practice his aim should obtain a [lighted] lantern, place it at a distance, pick up a weak and flexible bow, and take his position for shooting. If his method be to face the target obliquely, let him take his position obliquely; if his method be to face the target directly while seated with his legs crossed, let him so take his place and sit; and if his method be to face the target halfway between the oblique and frontal positions, let him so arrange himself. Then let him align the arrowhead with the flame and focus his sight upon it with whichever he desires of the methods and their different variations that are described above—closing one eye and opening the other or opening them both—and, drawing the limit of the arrow, continue so to practice until he arrives at the choice of method which is most attractive and best suited to himself.

There are two schools of thought upon focusing the sight upon the target. One insists on doing so at the very beginning, and on continuing to maintain and adjust it throughout the draw until the moment of release. The second ignores focusing the sight at the beginning, but takes it up sometime during the draw or toward its end.

The first is the method of those who face the target directly and has two variations. The first consists of aligning the arrowhead with the target, focusing the sight thereon, adjusting the left arm and the right elbow so that they may be straight and level with each other, and drawing steadily without haste or languor until the full length of the arrow is reached; then release.

The second consists of deferring the focusing of the sight upon the target until half or two thirds of the arrow has been drawn, whereupon the sight is focused and the arrow is given a sudden jerk backward until its entire length is drawn. It is then released. This is the better and more accurate of the two variations, both of which are used by those who face the target directly.

The second method is used by those who face the target obliquely, and it also has two variations. The first consists of ignoring the aim until all but the width of one fist in the length of the arrow has been drawn, when the archer pauses for a count of one, gives the arrow a sudden jerk backward—thereby completing the draw—and then releases.

This method is very good for warfare because the bow may be concealed from the enemy while most of the draw is being made. When a point the width of a fist from the arrowhead is reached, the arrow is turned toward the enemy, given a sudden jerk backward to complete the draw, and finally released.

The second variation consists of aiming first and then drawing up to the width of a fist from the arrowhead, when the aim is taken again and is followed by a sudden jerk backward to complete the draw. The arrow is then released. This is indeed the best method and is suitable for all purposes.

In describing how to aim at the target, archers have followed two different schools of thought:

One advocates the oblique position, which consists of looking at the target with the left eye in relation to the knuckles of the left hand. In the case of a short range the archer should look at the target from above the third knuckle of the index finger of his left hand. If the arrow then falls short because of the lightness of the bow or the heaviness of the arrow or the weakness of the archer himself, he should raise the third knuckle of his index finger into alignment with the target. If the range be long and the bow strong, he should aim at the target in the same manner as prescribed for the short range. If the arrow then falls short because of its weight or because of the weakness of the archer or because of the long range, he should align the third knuckle of his index finger with the target. If the arrow should again fall short, he should raise his left hand a little and look at the target from between the two knuckles at the base of the index finger and middle finger. If the arrow once more falls short, he should raise his left hand a little more and look at the target from the point bisecting the knuckle at the base of his middle finger. If the arrow should again fall short, let him look at the target from between the two knuckles at the base of his middle finger and ring finger. If the arrow should still fall short, he should raise his left hand a little more and look at the target from between the two knuckles at the base of the ring finger and the little finger. If the arrow should even yet fall short, he should raise his left hand further and look at the target from his forearm. If the arrow should exceed the mark, he should bring his left hand downward little by little, just as we have described in the case of raising it.

It has also been said that the archer may fix his aim by means of the fingers of his left hand by pointing the arrowhead at the center of the target. If the arrow should then fall short, he should raise his hand and align the index finger with the top of the target. If the arrow should again fall short, he should align the middle finger with the top of the target. If the arrow should still fall short, he should align the ring finger with the top of the target. If the arrow should again fall short, let him align the little finger with the top of the target. Finally, if the arrow should even yet fall short, he should align his forearm with the top of the target. If the arrow should exceed the mark, he must bring his left hand downward little by little, just as we have described in the case of raising it.

The second school of aiming advocates directly facing the target. In this method the archer places the last knuckle of the thumb of the left hand on a level with the left elbow when he stretches out his left arm for aiming. He then depends upon his wrist to adjust the excess or deficiency of the cast of the arrow, as well as upon holding the lower *siyah* of the bow out or in. Thus, if the arrow should fall short, he must bring the lower *siyah* out to the left and push with his wrist enough to insure sending the arrow close to the mark.[23] If, however, the arrow should fly beyond the mark, he must bring the lower *siyah* in to his side. This method is common to those who aim from the inside of the bow and to those who aim from the outside.

XX. On the loose or release

According to expert archers there are three ways of loosing the arrow. These are described as sprung (*mukhtalas*), twisted (*mafrūk*), and outstretched (*mutamaṭṭi*).

The sprung loose consists in drawing the arrow up to a point the width of a fist from its head, pausing for a count of one, and then loosing by pulling it back to its full length with force and speed and releasing with a jerk the

[23] This means that the head of the arrow is to be raised by bending the hand upward at the wrist.

index finger and thumb from the inside of the bow. The archer's arms are then relaxed and the bowstring turned downward toward the earth.

The twisted loose consists in drawing the arrow to its full length, pausing for a count of two, giving the arrow a twist with the right hand from the inside of the string, and then releasing the index finger and thumb and relaxing the hands. The twist (*farkah*) consists of pressing lightly upon the string with the base of the index finger and turning the right hand a little until the space between the thumb and index finger adheres to the side of the archer's neck, and, as it were, rubs against it.

The outstretched loose consists in drawing the arrow steadily to its full length, without any twist or inclination upward or downward and without haste or languor. When the arrowhead reaches the thumb the archer should loose without stop or pause. Others hold that he should pause for a count of two and then loose with a jerk from the inside of the string by releasing the index finger and thumb and relaxing the hands. This method is suitable for those who aim from the inside of the bow. The twist is suitable for those who aim from both the inside and the outside of the bow simultaneously. The spring is good for those who aim from the outside of the bow only.

There is no disagreement at all among the experts that the jerk[24] of the string should be done with force and speed and without slowness or delay, because the strength and velocity depend upon the speed of the loose, upon which depends the secret of all shooting.

An expert archer has said that a strong archer looses at

[24] While "jerk" does not convey the exact meaning of the original because it suggests inaccuracy, a better word does not come readily to mind. The central idea of most of these descriptions of drawing and loosing is that the archer may take as much time as he wishes in pulling back most of the arrow, but for the last few inches he must be quick and he must finally loose in a snappy manner without letting the string creep or his fingers drag.

the full draw without stop, delay, or pause, while a weak archer does not loose until he has drawn the arrow for its full length and has rested his hand upon his shoulder. This is because, in the case of the strong archer, from the commencement of the draw to its very conclusion, his hand remains in the same position as when he first took his aim; that is, he sustains his aim from beginning to end. This is not true of the weak archer, as his aim is not taken until he has brought the arrow to a pause with its head held against the *kabid* and has rested his hand upon his shoulder.

In the opinion of the author, the merit of this is questionable, for how could a weak archer take his aim during the pause when his arrow is full drawn and his hand is resting on his shoulder, if he were already proven unable to focus his aim at a time when he was free of strain and stress, namely, at the commencement of the draw and up to the moment of loosing?

This method is that of the followers of the intermediate school, who hold that the archer should pause for a period ranging between the counts of two and ten. This period is highly strenuous and the aim taken then is most difficult. Consequently, it would be better if the weak archer did not try to pause at the full draw. He should wait neither a little nor much, but should develop the knack of taking aim immediately at the conclusion of the draw, because he cannot keep his left arm steady from the beginning to the end of the operation. The strong archer, however, can pause to his heart's content. Pausing at the conclusion of the draw is, in fact, very good. Its duration is said to be at least the count of three, or, according to others, until the face is flushed with blood.

The release consists of opening the hands of the archer, while, at the same time, he separates them from each other by endeavoring, if possible, to make the ends of his shoulder blades meet in the center of his back. If the archer cannot accomplish that, let him try his best to approximate such a meeting by releasing both hands simultaneously. He should beware of releasing one hand before the other or of releasing the one and leaving the other unreleased. Some archers are wont to reach the back of the ear when releasing the right hand and likewise when releasing the left.[25]

Al-Ṭabari warned against releasing one hand and leaving the other unreleased, lest the archer lose his aim, spoil his shot, scatter his arrows, and disturb his accuracy. Even though he might hit the mark while releasing one hand before the other, his method would not be good and he would not be considered an archer by experts, nor would his shooting be dependable. He scores a hit simply by persistent practice, and if ever he should neglect to shoot for a few days his accuracy would disappear, in contrast to that of the archer who releases his hands simultaneously. The latter may stay away from his practice for several days but on his return to it little disparity is evident. Such a person is numbered among archers by the experts.

Consequently, the simultaneous release of both hands at the moment of shooting is an important principle of marksmanship. It has already been mentioned among the princi-

[25] To the layman, this releasing of both hands by making the shoulder blades meet may sound like nonsense. If taken too literally perhaps it is, but to the practical archer it is quite intelligible. The prime requisite in loosing is to create as little disturbance as possible in one's artillery (*see I Samuel 20:40*) while keeping it at the highest potential of efficiency. This is accomplished by maintaining absolute steadiness of the hands and arms while the shoulder blades are slightly approximated. Of course they cannot really be made to touch each other, but they feel as if they were going to do so, and, as a result of their contraction, the tension between the hands is increased just enough to pull the string off the fingers if the clench is not simultaneously strengthened. While the idea of releasing the right hand is clear to anyone, that of releasing the left is more obscure. It is true that many of the best modern archers allow a free movement of the bow handle within the grasp of the left hand at the exact moment of loosing and this, with the consequent "follow up" or sustained tension of the bow hand is apparently what the author means. At the end of Section XVI he suggested it as used by the Persians. Yet many an equally good archer never relaxes his grasp but holds on like a vise to the very end of the loose. If the author also had this mode in mind, he must have referred to the preservation of tension or the "follow-up" when he wrote of the release of the left hand.

ples and is a procedure agreed upon by all experts. It should, therefore, be strictly observed without any neglect or omission.

XXI. On the passage of the arrow over the left hand

According to the experts, the passage of the arrow over the left hand may follow one of four different ways: first, letting it pass over the knuckle of the thumb; second, letting it pass over the index finger; third, letting it pass over the upper part of the nail of the thumb by holding the thumb straight and placing the index finger beneath it as though one were locking his fingers for thirteen; fourth, letting it pass over the tips of the index finger and thumb as though one were locking his fingers for thirty.

The first, namely, letting the arrow pass over the knuckle of the thumb, is very bad because it is not free from the danger of cutting the skin with the feathers; or the arrow itself may strike the thumb and wound it. The second, namely, letting it pass over the index finger, is slightly better than the first. Both are the methods of those who hold the grip straight, but they are, however, no good.

The third, in which the arrow passes over the upper part of the thumb, as though the fingers were locking thirteen, is the method of those who hold the grip obliquely and is followed by most of the archers of Khurasan. It is, however, very bad because the archer using it holds the grip very obliquely and keeps his thumb straight, with the result that if he should incline the bow a little in order to obtain a clear view of the target the arrow would fall off the nail. It is still worse in warfare because it does not insure a hit, as the arrow is apt to fall or not be in the correct position. It is better, therefore, to avoid the use of this way completely.

The fourth, namely, letting the arrow pass over the bases of the nails of the index finger and thumb, as though the fingers were locked for thirty, is the method of the intermediate school and is by far the best and safest.

XXII. On blisters and wounds on the index finger of the right hand caused by stringing, clenching, drawing and loosing, together with the remedies thereof

THE index finger of the right hand may receive blisters and wounds from either of two things. The first is dependence upon the index finger and thumb for pushing the eye of the string into the nock while bracing a bow. Here the projecting edge of the upper *siyah* may eat into the index finger. The other is the use of so strong a bow that the archer needs his entire hand to brace it and, in so doing, brings his index finger between the string and the edge of the *siyah*, where it is bruised. Both are, therefore, the result of the same cause, namely, the pinching of the index finger between the string and the narrow edge of the *siyah* because of the archer's endeavoring either to brace a bow which is well within his strength by pushing on the eye instead of by bending the bow further, or by bracing a bow which is too strong for him and therefore requires the pressure of his whole hand.

All such injury can be avoided if the archer will depend solely on the palm of his hand for pressing against the bow and will use his index finger and thumb for nothing else than pushing the eye of the string into the nock by the easy and effortless technique which has been described in the section on stringing. If the bow be too strong for him to brace, he had better let it go; but if he *must* brace it, he had better wrap a rag around his hand before making the attempt. However, none of these difficulties will befall the archer who knows the exact manner of stringing and practices it regularly.

The base of the index finger may be blistered or wounded when drawing because of either of two things: first, the placing of the string (during the operations of arranging the fingers and drawing) underneath the middle joint of the index finger; in other words, locking the fingers for twenty-three. This can be avoided by placing the string at the time of arranging the fingers between the lower and middle joints of the index finger; in other words, by locking the fingers for sixty-three.

The second cause of injury is pressing upon the string with the base of the index finger from the beginning of the draw until the time of loosing. This also is a result of locking twenty-three. It can be avoided by keeping the base of the index finger off the string by locking sixty-three and by refraining from pressing with the finger until the time of loosing, as the archer may then do if he chooses this method, which is known as the twist.

The tip of the index finger may be blistered or wounded from the blow of the string because of any one of six things. The first is bad loosing, wherein the archer releases his thumb sooner than his index finger. It can be avoided by releasing the index finger before the thumb. The second is the strength of the bow. The third is weakness of the archer. Both the second and third can be resolved to one principle, namely, the inability of the archer to wield the bow, either because of its strength or because of his own weakness. The fourth is extreme cold. The fifth is excessive heat, which causes the hand to perspire. All but the first can be overcome at the time of arranging the fingers by placing the index finger over the thumb from the outside of the string if the lock be oblique. But if the archer does not follow the oblique method of locking, or clenching, his hold on the string will then be weak because he must depend for drawing solely upon his thumb, without the aid of the index finger. Such a method may also blister and wound the thumb, and even cause its tip under the nail to become black with congealed blood. The sixth thing which may cause an injury to the index finger is the lock of twenty-three, which has the effect of lengthening the index finger and exposing it to the blows of the string.

XXIII. On the blow of the string on the archer's right thumb, which causes it to turn black and blue on the inside and beneath the nail and sometimes results in breaking the nail; as well as on the blistering and bruising of the left thumb at the time of shooting, together with the remedies thereof

The string may hit the right thumb of the archer because of bad loosing, wherein the archer leaves his thumb folded to his palm. It can be avoided by opening the thumb fully to its back.

The tip of the thumb may turn black and blue because of two things. The first is the rubbing of the string over it at the time of loosing. This can be avoided by opening the thumb fully to its back. The second is the placing of the string between the crease of the knuckle and the end of the thumb, with the result that the blood clots in the tip and turns it black and blue. This can be avoided by placing the string close to the groove if, indeed, the archer's method be not that of placing it directly in the groove itself.

The nail of the right thumb may turn black and blue or even be broken because of one of four things. The first is the placing of the index finger upon the nail of the thumb and the string upon the flesh opposite as the archer locks his fingers in the clench. The pressure of the draw will then fall upon the nail and the blood may clot under it or it may even be broken. This can be prevented by placing the index finger upon the back of the thumb just below the nail and upon one third of the nail.[26]

The second cause of injury is releasing the thumb sooner than the index finger at the moment of loosing, with the result that the finger rubs heavily on the nail and causes it to become black and blue or even to break. This can be avoided by releasing the index finger sooner than the thumb. The third is the rubbing of the thumb stall against the string; and the fourth is either an excessively long thumb stall or one that is too short.

The thumb of the left hand may be blistered or wounded, when the arrow is loosed, in any one of three places: on the lower phalanx, on the upper phalanx, and on the flesh projecting from between the bases of the index finger and thumb.

The injury to the lower phalanx of the thumb may result from one of three things: first, from too thin a grip and too large a hand; second, from a poor manner of grasping the grip; third, from greater stiffness in the bending of the lower limb which consequently overbalances the upper limb.

These can be remedied as follows: in the case of the thin grip by wrapping a tape of leather or cotton around the grip; in the case of the poor manner of grasping the grip by rectifying it according to the directions given in Section XVI; in the case of imbalance by warming the lower limb a little over a slow fire until it is corrected, if the difference be small, or by reducing it with a file if the fire should fail to rectify it.

26 This breaking of the nail probably does not mean a splitting of the nail itself, which we have never seen, but a separation of the nail from the matrix at the cuticle. This accident to fingernails has often occurred in our experience on American shooting fields, and many such injured men have courageously shot out the match in spite of agonizing pain.

Injury to the upper phalanx of the thumb may result from any one of three things: from rigidity of the thumb and index finger while grasping the grip; from raising the upper phalanx of the thumb while drawing; and from placing the thumb upon the index finger while performing the same operation of drawing.

These can be remedied by relaxing the thumb and index finger if they be rigid; by lowering the upper phalanx of the thumb if it be raised; and by evening up the index finger and thumb if the latter be placed upon the former, so that they will then form the lock of thirty.

Injury to the flesh projecting at the base of the left thumb and index finger may result from one of three things: from wrongly holding the grip hard and deep into the palm; from nocking the arrow too low on the string; and from too small and narrow a nock in the arrow.

These can be remedied by rectifying the hold on the grip in accordance with the manner described in Section XVI, by nocking the arrow higher on the string, and by enlarging the nock of the arrow if it be too small.

The flesh at the base of the thumb and index finger may be injured from roughness of the feathers. This can be avoided by nocking the arrow a little higher on the string.

XXIV. On the blow of the string on the forearm of the archer and the remedy thereof

THE forearm of the archer may be hit by the string in one of three places: on the front of the forearm just below the elbow; on the wrist bone next to the little finger; and just next to the wrist bone.[27]

[27] At this point it seems pertinent to scan the general skeletal anatomy of the forearm, wrist, and hand in order to harmonize the conceptions of the author with our own. The forearm contains two bones, the ulna and the radius. The former is big at the upper end, where it forms the elbow

The forearm just below the elbow may be hit because of one of three things: because of the strength of the bow and the weakness of the archer; because of poor drawing, wherein the archer draws along the length of his arm; and because of a dangling sleeve.

These can be remedied in the case of too strong a bow by using one which the archer can draw without any effort or strain; in the case of the poor method of drawing by correcting the draw; in the case of the dangling garment by turning up the sleeve.

The wrist bone next to the little finger may be hit because of one of three things also: first, because of holding the grip too high in the palm, thereby causing it to be at a distance from the wrist so that the front of the wrist is pushed into the bow;[28] second, because of too long a string; third, because of an irregularity in the lower limb.

These can be remedied by rectifying the manner of holding the grip, in the case of the wrist's being pushed into the bow; by shortening the string if it is too long; and by removing the irregularity of the lower limb according to the instructions given in the preceding section if it suffers from any lack of balance.

by articulating with the humerus of the upper arm, but it tapers down to hardly more than a point at the lower end, where it forms little more than a side flange to the wrist joint. The radius is very small at the upper end, where it is attached to the ulna in a free manner which permits the hand to be turned on either its palm or back, but at the lower end it is very large and forms nearly the whole width of the wrist.

In the wrist itself are eight small bones called carpals which look like irregular pebbles and which move on each other to varying extent. Beyond them lie the five metatarsals, one for each finger, forming the solid part of the hand.

Although the flexibility of the wrist is due to the great number of joints between so many bones, it is commonly called the wrist joint—not joints—even by doctors. Apparently its complex structure was not understood by our Arabic author, and by "wrist bone" he usually means the bases of the first or fifth metacarpals with, possibly, the two carpals with which they are principally joined. Thus, he often means what we would think of as part of the hand rather than wrist.

28 "Into the bow" means between the bow and string, the idea being that the hand is bent back at the wrist.

The archer's forearm may be hit by the string next to the wrist bone because of one of eight things: thickness of the string; excessive flesh in the palm of the archer; a relaxed condition of his joints; thinness of the grip; crookedness in the grip or in the two *siyahs*; excessive cold; excessive heat; a loose hold on the grip.

These things can be remedied by making the string thinner if it be thick; by pressing the flesh of the palm if it be excessive; by relinquishing shooting until vigor and strength are regained if the joints happen to be relaxed because of temporary sluggishness; by improving the grip according to the instructions given in the preceding section if it be too thin; by holding the bow so that the width of one and a half fingers of the grip lie above the upper part of the wrist and the width of half a finger below the lower part. If excess of heat or cold be the cause, the remedy lies in wrapping a piece of scraped leather around the grip. This will warm the hand in the case of cold and will absorb its perspiration in the case of heat.

If a loose hold on the grip be the cause, the remedy will lie in tightening the hold.

XXV. On the blow of the string on the chin of the archer, or on his ear, and the remedies thereof

THE chin of the archer may be hit by the string because of one of seven things: a feeble loose; inclination of the upper *siyah* toward the arrow; projection of the lower part of the bow beyond the right measure; playing with his head when his hand reaches his shoulder during the draw; sticking his chin toward the string; pressing his right hand against his face; and too strong a bow.

These can be remedied by carefully avoiding their causes. Should the hitting persist, it will do so because of the ignorance of the archer, in which case he should turn his face a little away from the string, even though this is an acknowledged fault, and should endeavor both to rectify anything wrong, or better, scrupulously to avoid it. When he has finally mastered all these things, he should discontinue the practice of turning his face away from the string because, as we have already mentioned, that practice is a fault.

XXVI. When the tip of the bow hits the ground at the moment of loosing, and the remedy thereof

THE bowtip may hit the ground especially when the archer is seated for shooting. This may be because of one of four things: bending the greater part of the body over the bow; poor sitting, wherein the archer bears his weight upon both legs; too strong a bow, which causes him to employ his body for drawing, with the result that the bow draws him more than he draws it; and allowing his left hand to prevail over his right.

These things can be remedied by elevating the target in the case of bending over the bow with the body; by correcting the posture, in the case of poor sitting, by unfolding the left leg and stretching it and relying upon the right leg for support; by substituting a lighter and weaker bow if the bow is too strong; and finally, if the left hand prevails over the right, by practicing with the "limbering" instrument devised by experts for training and strengthening the drawing hand. This instrument has been described in the section "On ascertaining the weight of a bow" [Section IX].

XXVII. When the nock of the arrow breaks and the remedy thereof

THE nock of the arrow may break in one of two ways: it may either split in two and break, or its right lip may break. It may split in two because of the narrowness of its notch throughout its depth and the thickness of the string, or because of the narrowness of its lower part so that the string fails to reach its bottom; instead, it breaks under the thickness and pressure of the string. This can be remedied by enlarging the nock with the aid of a file. Breaking the right side or lip of the nock is a grave blemish, and occurs only to ignorant beginners. It can be remedied by relaxing the pressure of the base of the index finger on the nock and by discontinuing to exert any weight thereupon.

XXVIII. On causing the arrow to move on itself, or wag, in its flight

THE arrow is moved on its flight by one of thirty-five things; six are imparted by the archer, eight by the bow, nine by the string, and twelve by the arrow itself.

The six imparted by the archer are: pressing against the nock of the arrow with the base of the index finger from the commencement of the draw to the moment of loosing; removing the bottom of the nock away from the string during the draw and the loose; a bad loose; shooting against the wind; a loose hold on the grip; weakness of the archer and excessive weakness of the bow.

The eight imparted by the bow are: disparity in the two *siyahs* of the bow, the one being of hard wood and the other of soft wood; the intrusion of the lower limb upon the upper limb;[29] a crooked grip; a crooked limb, whether the upper or the lower; thin and crooked *siyahs*; too long a bow for the archer; too strong a bow for the archer and too light an arrow; and too light a bow and too heavy an arrow.

The nine imparted by the string are: too long a string; too thick a string and too narrow a nock; too thin a string and too large a nock; disparity in the size of the eyes of the string, the one being too small and the other too large; oversize of the two eyes of the string; thickness of the upper part of the string and thinness of the lower part; thinness of the upper part of the string and thickness of the lower part; and the string's being too light for the bow.

The twelve imparted by the arrow itself are: disparity in the weight of its feathers, some being heavy and some being light; some of the feathers being too high and others being too low; too much feathering; too little feathering; the loss of some of the feathers; too large a nock; a split or hole in the body of the arrow; a heavy stele and a light arrowhead; a light stele and a heavy arrowhead; a crooked arrow; too light an arrowhead and too many feathers; too heavy an arrowhead and too few feathers.

The arrow may move on itself in one of seven ways: it

[29] The Arabic expression which is translated "the intrusion of the lower limb upon the upper limb," is without a literal equivalent in English. It may also be translated as "the predominance of the lower limb over the upper limb," and as "the prevalence of the lower limb." It occurs in several places in the manuscript and seems to mean that the lower limb—being shorter than the upper limb—may also, in such cases as are under consideration, be stronger than the upper limb. In some sentences it is freely translated so as to indicate that fact. If such an imbalance exists, then—in the highly reflexed and delicately balanced composite bow—the lower limb will remain much less bent when the bow is strung and consequently will be closer to the string; thus making the string lie at an angle to the grip instead of correctly parallel. The stronger limb will also resume its original status, or return to rest, more quickly than the weaker limb, and, for that reason, will not only cause the bow to kick in the hand but will so jerk the string as to produce an unbalanced propulsive impact on the arrow. The effects attributed to this "prevalence," or "intrusion" of strength, can be explained by this interpretation.

may wag from the moment it leaves the bow to the moment it alights on the target; it may leave the bow wagging until it reaches half the range, when it will become steady and travel the remaining half of the range straight until it falls on the target; or it may wag in exactly the opposite fashion, namely, it may leave the bow straight and accurately pointed until it reaches half the range, when it will swerve and wag until it falls; or it may swerve and gad toward the right; or toward the left; or it may leave the bow and travel straight until it reaches the end of the range, when it will swerve and wag; or it may swerve throughout its flight.

The arrow may move on itself from the time it leaves the bow until it alights on the target for one of seven reasons: crookedness in the arrow; lightness or heaviness in its feathers; the height of some of its feathers and the lowness of others; lightness of the arrowhead with excessive feathering; heaviness of the arrowhead with inadequacy of the feathers; narrowness of the nock and thickness of the string, which cause the arrow to leave the string draggingly; weakness of the archer; poorness of the loose; and weakness of the bow itself.

The arrow which leaves the bow moving, or wagging, until it has reached half the range, but then becomes steady and travels the remaining distance straight until it falls, may be influenced by one of three things: thinness and crookedness of the two *siyahs*; excessive pressure of the index finger against the nock and the string; and too strong a bow for the archer.

The arrow which leaves the bow straight and accurately pointed until it reaches half the range, but then swerves and wags, may be influenced by one of eight things: lightness of the arrow in proportion to the strength of the bow; oversize of the nock and thinness of the string; the presence of a hole or split in the arrow into which air may enter and cause the arrow to move on itself; a loose hold upon the grip at the time of the release; crookedness in the arrow either close to the nock or close to the arrowhead; greater strength in the lower limb than in the upper; oversize of one of the two eyes of the string; and crookedness of the grip or of one of the two arms.

The arrow which gads or wags and swerves either to the right or to the left may be influenced by one of two things: first, the feathers and the poorness of the draw—for the archer may draw toward the right and the feathers be on the left side, or toward the left and the feathers be on the right side—so that the arrow is shaken because of the poorness of the draw and swerves to the side on which the feathers are; or, second, the height of the upper bowtip in relation to a low position of the hand.

The arrow which moves on itself as it approaches the target may do so from one of eight things: crookedness in the arrow, either near the nock or near the head; lightness of the arrow; too large a nock; a concealed hole or split in the arrow; a loose hold upon the grip at the moment of release; a slight preponderance of the lower limb over the upper; too large eyes in the string; and an apparent crookedness in the grip.

The arrow moves on itself toward the end of its flight and not at the beginning because the disturbing factor fails to make itself evident until the greater part of the momentum has been expended. At the beginning of flight it travels straight because of the power of the bow and the strength of discharge, but when it approaches the mark those forces diminish, making it possible for the swerving factor to manifest itself. On the other hand, an arrow wags first and steadies itself last because the two *siyahs* are crooked and therefore discharge the arrow unevenly and cause it to wag, but, as it proceeds and the disturbing factor diminishes in power, it becomes steady and travels straight for the remaining distance.

Similarly, if the base of the index finger presses too hard

against the nock, the arrow is slightly bent and will emerge disturbed and unevenly. As it reaches the middle of the range, the disturbing factor diminishes in strength and the arrow regains its straight course. Likewise, in the case of a weak archer with too strong a bow, certain factors disturb the arrow at the commencement of its flight but, as they diminish, the arrow resumes its straight course. Let the archer therefore avoid using a bow the weight of which is greater than his strength warrants.

XXIX. On the management of the arrow when shooting against the wind, *et cetera*, and on trying not to shoot it when a break is found after it has been fully drawn

If the arrowhead is heavy and the feathers light, lower the nock and raise the head. It will then travel straight. If, on the other hand, its feathers are heavy and the arrowhead light, raise the nock and lower the head. It will then travel straight. If one of the feathers is heavy and the others light, hold the arrow in such a position as will have the heavy feather down and the light ones up. It will then travel straight. If, on the other hand, one of the feathers is light and the others are heavy, hold the arrow in such a position as will have the light feather up and the heavy ones down. It will then travel straight.

If the male feather (*dhakar*)[80] should drop off but the side feathers remain, you may shoot therewith and the arrow will travel straight because the loss of the male feather will do no harm. If, however, one of the side feathers should be lost, do not shoot; because an arrow in that condition will never travel straight.

[80] See Appendix, 5. The Male Feather.

If the arrow has no feathers at all and its head is light, there is no use in shooting; but, if its head is heavy, take a small piece of compactly woven rag, split it into three dangling parts still held together at one end, form a small hole in this intact portion, fit it around the arrow in place of the feathers, tie it firmly with a piece of twine, and shoot. The arrow will travel straight.

Wind invariably spoils and obstructs good shooting; consequently, avoid shooting in the wind. If you happen to be shooting when the wind starts to blow, stop until it subsides.

If you are shooting for a wager or trophy and your adversary insists upon continuing, you may, if the wind is blowing with you from behind, lean on your left leg because it offers a slower arrow; but beware of leaning on your right leg because it raises the flight of the arrow, causing it to be carried by the wind and go astray. Then hold your right hand firm, lower your left hand a little, and press with the thenar eminence against the grip. If, however, the wind is blowing from above, lean on your right leg, hold your left hand firm, lower your right hand a little, and press with your hypothenar eminence against the grip. This completely reverses the other performance.

If the wind blows from your right, turn your bow a little to the outside [the left], and aim at the lower edge of the target. If it blows from your left, do the reverse, namely, turn your bow a little to the inside [the right], and aim at the upper edge of the target.

If the wind blows from in front of you, raise your left hand a little since the wind will counteract the velocity of the arrow and its force will slow down the flight, with the result that the cast will be lessened.

When a person nocks an arrow in order to shoot down an enemy, and upon completing a full draw discovers in it a crack or break, he cannot very well use that arrow; for if he shoots it anyway it will be ineffective and the enemy will not only despise him but will lose no time in shooting him. If, on the other hand, he discards the broken arrow by letting it down, the enemy will shoot him before he can adjust another. He should therefore do his best to get rid of the arrow by folding his left index finger over it to hold it firmly, while the right hand draws the string further until it is clear of the nock. By this the enemy is led to believe that the arrow has been shot and is flying toward him, and, consequently becomes involved in an attempt to either dodge it or deflect it with his shield. While he is so busied, the archer quickly picks out another arrow, nocks it, and shoots. Or, if he so wishes, he may draw the string clear of the nock, shove the arrow to the ground with his chin, quickly take another, nock, and shoot it.

XXX. On how near or how far the target should be

ARCHERS throughout the world are agreed that the shortest practical range is twenty-five cubits and the longest is one hundred and twenty-five cubits; while the limit beyond which no accurate shooting is possible is three hundred cubits. One archer has stated that the best range should measure forty-five bow-lengths, and that anyone who shoots beyond that limit commits a mistake; but he failed to mention whether the bow should be braced or unbraced when measuring out the course. If it were braced, the distance would be roughly one hundred and twenty-five cubits, which is exactly what we have said before; but if it were unbraced, the distance would be one hundred and forty cubits, assuming that the length of the bow is three cubits and one finger.[81]

Whether the bow is self or composite, the relative range remains the same in length or shortness. This will be dis-

[81] See Appendix, 6. The Cubit.

cussed later under a special section where we shall show that the variations in the length and shortness of the bow depend upon the size of the archer himself. In fact, no one is known to have shot beyond forty-five bow-lengths and to have still remained accurate, since then he is compelled to raise his left hand in order that the arrow may reach the target, with the result that the bow is held high and his sight low, thereby making his aim a matter of guessing and approximation. Furthermore, his arrow, on leaving the bow, rises above it as much as the stature of a man or more, and falls on the target obliquely from above; which is considered by experts to be a grave blemish.

The reason which made experts hold that correct shooting is limited to a range of forty-five bow-lengths was experience, which showed that the arrow then left the bow straight—neither rising above nor falling below until it hit the mark or approached it. However, an arrow in flight should rise above the ground half a bow-length over and above the distance between the upper bow-tip and the ground—this being in the case of the sitting archer—thereby assuring a straight course without rising high or falling low. This is one of the main secrets of the profession of archery, though it has been forgotten by many an archer and still many more have never even known it, so that only a few are aware of it.

The soundness of this theory of a range of forty-five bow-lengths has been established and its superiority and excellence have been proven. Its advocates do not permit shooting beyond that distance. As a matter of fact, it is less than half the limit of possible effective range, although, according to experts, no accuracy is sure beyond it.

Those who have permitted shooting the limit of possible effectiveness, which is three hundred cubits, have done so on the assumption that strong and heavy bows are capable of casting arrows straight for that distance—without rising high or dropping low—especially when the archers who wield them follow the method of not raising the hand for a distant target nor dropping it for a near one, but rectify any error in shooting—whether on the excessive side or on the short side—by projecting the lower *siyah* of the bow to the left if they desire an increase of cast, or by bringing it in toward the side if they desire a decrease. But those who follow the method of raising the hand in order to counteract, or compensate for, any possibility of the arrow's falling short of the mark, or of dropping the hand to avoid its going beyond, hold that aiming along the arm and locked fingers is just as good as aiming along the arrowhead and is unaffected by dropping the sight. One flaw, however, appears in the method; namely, that the arrow falls on the target obliquely from above and rests thereon as though it were dangling. This is unacceptable in tournaments.

Abu-Hāshim al-Māwardi and Isḥāq al-Raqqi held that the way to correct the error of excess or loss in the range is by raising the left hand in the case of loss, when the arrow falls short of the target, and by lowering it in the case of excess, when the arrow falls beyond the target.

If you have a strong bow which weighs two hundred rotls,[82] and wish to shoot a distance of three hundred cubits, you should align your little finger with the top of the target; if you wish to shoot a distance of two hundred and fifty cubits, you should align your ring finger with the top of the target; if you wish to shoot a distance of two hundred cubits, you should align your middle finger with the top of the target; if you wish to shoot a distance of one hundred and fifty cubits, you should align your index finger with the top of the target; if you wish to shoot a distance of one hundred and twenty-five cubits, you should align the arrowhead with the center of the target.

If your bow weighs a hundred rotls or more, but less than two hundred rotls, and you wish to shoot a distance

[82] See Appendix, 7. Weights of Bows.

of three hundred cubits, you should align your left forearm with the top of the target; if you wish to shoot a distance of two hundred and fifty cubits, you should align your little finger with the top of the target; if you wish to shoot a distance of two hundred cubits, you should align your ring finger with the top of the target; if you wish to shoot a distance of one hundred and fifty cubits, you should align your middle finger with the top of the target; if you wish to shoot a distance of one hundred cubits, you should align the part between the knuckles of the base of the index finger and the middle finger with the top of the target; if you wish to shoot a distance between fifty and twenty-five cubits, you should align the arrowhead with the center of the target.[38]

If, either because of the strength of the bow or because of the shortness of the range or because of both, the arrow should fall beyond the target, you should lower your left hand gradually according to the gradations already mentioned. If, either because of the weakness of the bow or because of the length of the range or because of both, it should fall short of the target, you should raise your left hand gradually according to the same gradations.

Ṭāhir al-Balkhi maintained that the way to correct any excess or loss in the range of the arrow was by bringing the lower *siyah* in toward his side in the case of excess, and by raising the bow with his wrist in the case of loss; or, by raising the bow with his wrist and projecting the lower *siyah* away from his side if the loss persisted, without resorting to the device of raising the left hand in the case of loss in the range of the arrow or dropping it in the case of excess therein. Instead, he would hold the last knuckle of the thumb of his left hand on a level with his left shoulder when he stretched out his left arm for aiming, and would correct any error therein by bringing the lower *siyah* in toward his side to an extent which would rectify the error

[38] See Appendix, 8. Sighting and Range.

and bring the arrow closer to the target in the case of excess, and by pushing out the bow with his wrist in the case of loss. If the arrow still fell short of the target, he would push the bow out with his wrist and project the lower *siyah* away from his side to an extent which would rectify the error and bring the arrow closer to the target.

All this can be done only after determining the weight of the bow; whether it is light or heavy and how much in either case.

Ṭāhir al-Balkhi declared that experts are agreed that the top of the target (*qirṭās*) is the central point on its upper edge; but I say that its top is the extreme point of its upper right corner because, when the archer aligns the hand which holds the arrow with the upper right corner of the target, his left hand will be in line with the central point.

Some experts have said that this method of shooting is good only for those who aim from the inside of the bow and is useless for those who aim from the outside.

XXXI. On standing and sitting for aiming

STANDING for aiming may be done in three different ways: acute obliqueness[34] wherein the mark is in line with the left shoulder, which is the method of abu-Hāshim

[34] The Arabic words which are translated as "acute obliqueness" indicate the position, or standing, of the archer, which in England and America is known as *sideways*. In it, the archer's two shoulders are in line with the mark, or target, and his head is turned sharp to the left to bring the right eye into the direction of aim. The greatest reach is obtained by this method because of the full extension of the bow arm, and the greatest strength can be applied because traction is made by the powerful muscles of the shoulders and back—very much as in swimming by the breast stroke—and not by the weaker muscles and more constricted movements of the arms; all of which seems to have been understood by abu-Hāshim and the author. The reader can see the possibilities in himself by extending his left arm first to the left and then to the front and noting the difference in the distances between his hand and right eye.

al-Māwardi; direct facing of the mark wherein it lies, as it were, between the eyes, which method is called the *Khusruwāni* and is the way of Ṭāhir al-Balkhi; and a position halfway between acute obliqueness and direct facing, in which the mark is in line with the left eye, this being the method of Isḥāq al-Raqqi.

The reason for these variations is the desire for effective strength and deadliness. Said God: "Make ready against them what force ye can." This was interpreted by the Prophet to mean shooting with the bow and arrow. Those who advocate the position of acute obliqueness maintain that it offers greater strength and deadliness than either of the two other positions, because it makes possible a longer draw, a stronger bow, and the most powerful and effective shot. Furthermore, he who uses this position can protect himself with a shield, which he can hold while shooting.

On the other hand, he who employs the frontal position of directly facing his opponent, shortens his draw and, consequently, weakens his shot. Furthermore, he cannot enjoy the protection of a shield while shooting but is compelled to take it off for the operation, thereby exposing himself to the enemy. Only after he has finished shooting can he reach for the shield and try to protect himself. The clumsiness and weakness of this is very clear. Strong and powerful shooting, as well as the safest protection against the enemy, are possible only in the oblique position. It is the correct method, advocated and used by abu-Hāshim.

Advocates of the frontal position, which is free from any obliqueness, maintain that it offers greater accuracy and, therefore, is more deadly. Furthermore, though its draw is short, it still has power, strength, and deadliness; for deadliness lies in accuracy. Again, one who follows the frontal position may protect himself with a coat of mail or two, which will not interfere with shooting. On the other hand, the use of a coat of mail will interfere with the shooting of one who follows the oblique position, since it will crowd the tip of the bow and militate against the accuracy of the shot. If the tip of the bow is projected away, the accuracy of the shot will be disturbed, and if it is brought in, the shield will interfere with it. Therefore, the frontal position is claimed to be deadlier because of its greater accuracy. It is the method of Ṭāhir.

Those who advocate the position halfway between the oblique and the frontal, maintain that it has the advantages of both and the shortcomings of neither. It combines a long draw, which insures power and strength[85] as well as deadliness, with protection through the use of shields and coats of mail without any fear of interference. This is the method of Isḥāq al-Raqqi.

There is a fourth position of standing for the aim, namely, standing with one's back to the mark and feet together in front; the archer then draws his arrow and turns, pivotlike, on his hips so as to face the mark. Throughout the operation his feet remain firmly planted together.

The oblique position of standing for the aim consists of presenting the left shoulder and left leg toward the mark, with the left fingers and toes in line with it, while the right leg is planted behind the left, firm and straight, and is separated from it by about the length of a cubit. This is an extremely good position for a warrior or for one who is climbing a hill or a mound or an elevation in the earth, since his legs would then correspond to his gait uphill, and, in the event of his tripping over a stone, he will then lean on his right leg.

Another way is exactly the opposite, wherein the archer extends his left leg and bears on the right, which he may move for walking. This method is good for an archer going down hill and is the reverse of the former method used for

[85] "Power and strength" are terms of such nearly identical meaning as to be difficult of interpretation. It seems to us that their intended significance is length of cast and force of impact.

going up hill. In either case, the feet should be about a cubit's length apart.

The frontal position, or direct facing of the target, consists in standing straight opposite the target, with the feet about a palm [four inches] apart, or perhaps a little less. This position is known as the *Khusruwāni*, and is good for a near target, trick shooting, and weak bows, because it offers a great deal of accuracy, though it is not so deadly as the other types.

The position halfway between the frontal and the oblique consists in putting forward the left arm toward the target, without either facing it frontally or obliquely, and aligning the target with the left eye, while the feet are about a span apart and the left is planted a little ahead of the right. This is by far the best standing position for warfare as well as for other purposes.

In sitting for aim there are also three positions: acute oblique, frontal, and in between. There are, however, five different manners of sitting.

One is to plant your feet apart and squat upon them while your legs [i.e., from ankle to knee] remain erect, spreading your knees somewhat as you bear down on your thighs. This position is the basis of all other sitting postures, and is good and suitable for all methods of shooting, namely, the oblique, the frontal, and the in between. It is used by most archers in Khurasan, Egypt, and other lands.

Another is to fold your right limb, planting its knee in the ground, hold your left leg [ankle to knee] erect, and sit leaning upon the left thigh. This posture was used by most of the ancient Persians and is that of the fleeing archer, or one who stealthily approaches his enemy or prey. If he views what he can shoot, he shoots it; otherwise he flees, starting from his left leg.

Still another is the exact reverse of the preceding posture, namely, to fold your left limb, planting its knee into the ground, hold your right leg erect and lean upon the right thigh. This is a good posture, especially for aiming with a strong bow, and is particularly suitable for beginners.

Another is one which resembles the standing posture and is called "the competitor's seat" (*jalsat al-muthāqif*).[36] It consists in bending the left leg [limb] with the knee toward the ground and keeping the right leg unbent, while the feet are separated by as much as the length of the shin bone, or a little less. Throughout the operation, the right leg offers the main support. This is indeed a good posture and is used by most of the archers of Andalusia.

Another posture is to sit with crossed legs facing the target. It is a good posture for near targets, trick shooting, and weak bows only, and is called "the king's posture."

Every manner of standing for shooting consists in keeping the legs straight and erect, without inclining either the body or the head, and without throwing either hip to the side or the buttocks backward.

XXXII. On the variations in the length and construction of the Arab bow

KNOW that the construction of the bow varies for three different things: places, individuals, and objects.

Regarding the variations in places: some archers maintain that the bow with which an archer shoots from above downward should have *siyahs* of equal size, that is, one not longer than the other; while the bow with which an archer shoots from below upward should have its lower *siyah* longer than the upper. Otherwise, its construction remains the same: uniform. This was described in the section on the

[36] Here, as elsewhere in the manuscript, the word "competitor" seems to mean *flight shooter*, that is, one who strives for distance and not for accuracy of aim. Similarly, "competition" and "competitive" will be found to refer to flight shooting.

different kinds of bows, where it was explained that the upper *siyah* of the bow together with the upper arm and the width of a finger on the grip constitute one half of the bow, while the remaining part of the grip with the lower arm and *siyah* make up the other half. Such is the verdict of the master archers.

The construction of the bow varies, too, in the prevalence of some of its parts over the others as a result of different climatic conditions. Thus, in regions extremely hot or extremely cold, as well as in places which are very damp and humid, the suitable bows are those which have abundant wood and wide limbs; whereas in regions of moderate heat, cold, and humidity, the suitable bows are those which have an abundance of sinew and narrow limbs. The latter are also suitable for use in moderate seasons, such as the spring. In regions the climate of which tends to be cold and damp, like Syria and Andalusia, the suitable bows are those which are scant in wood, abundant in horn, and moderate in sinew and glue.

The Bedouins of the Hijaz use nothing except bows made of *nab'*, or *shawḥaṭ*, or *shiryān* wood, while those who live near water and nearby groups back their bows with sinew and face them with goat horn, as we have already mentioned, because of the intense heat. According to some experts, bows made of *nab'*, *shawḥaṭ*, and *shiryān* wood are useless outside the Hijaz. Others have recommended that in countries of excessive heat the sinew should be saturated with glue made of the best parchment, which is characteristically moist and, therefore, suitable for hot regions but not for those which are cold and humid.

Variations in the construction of bows, because of the different archers who are to use them, are accounted for by the fact that experts have agreed that for each archer there is a particular bow best suited to his own build. They have also agreed that such a bow should be measured with relation to the arrow which is to be shot in it and that the individual archer is, in turn, the basis of that arrow. They have, however, disagreed concerning the ratio in length of the bow to the arrow, with some maintaining that the bow should be, when unstrung and measured from one extremity to the end of the horn of the other limb, the width of three fingers shorter than its arrow. This is the opinion of abu-Hāshim, who claims that the arrow of the short bow is quicker in release, stronger in hitting, and deadlier in aim. Others have maintained that the bow should be, when unstrung and measured from the end of one horn to the end of the other, exactly the length of the arrow.[87] This is the opinion of Ṭāhir and Isḥāq, who claim that if this portion of the unstrung bow were longer than the arrow such a length would militate against the cast of the arrow and the power of its impact. On the other hand, if it were shorter than the arrow, the strength of the bow would overcome the archer, who would then be unable to draw it to the full length of the arrow except with difficulty and with the result that his left arm would be shaken, his aim spoiled, and his effectiveness gone, since they depend on the ability of the archer to control his bow. Furthermore, no archer using too short a bow can ever operate it well; frequently it is broken or its strings snap.

Still others have maintained that the arrow should measure exactly the length of the strung bow; while some have said that the correct length of the arrow should be exactly that of the strung bow if the *siyahs* were long, and exactly that of the unstrung bow if they were short.[88] The ques-

[87] This measure includes the two flexible arms and the grip but excludes both *siyahs*. The one preferred by abu-Hāshim adds one *siyah* to this but subtracts the width of three fingers.

[88] The statement that an arrow might be as long as a bow could be made only if the bow were of the very short composite type. If the bow measured three cubits and a finger, of sixty-five inches, as is stated on page 77, an arrow of that length would be absurd. It would be equally absurd to say that the longest accurate range is forty-five bow lengths, if the bow were no longer than an arrow. The author seems to give without distinction the opinions of his several authorities, who, in one case, may have had in mind either the wooden bow or a backed one of similar pattern and, in

tion of the ratio of the length of the arrow to the stature of the individual archer will be discussed later under a special heading.

Variations in the construction of the bow in accordance with the different objects for which it is to be used result in five kinds of bows: a bow for warfare, another for training and practice, a third for target shooting, a fourth for competition, and a fifth for trick shooting.

The bow for warfare should be, in strength, equal to that of the archer himself, with short *siyahs*—lest they hit the shield or whatever the archer carries—and a straight grip. It should have more horn than wood and, likewise, more sinew than wood. Furthermore, it should not be excessive in recurvature, so that it may be quickly strung and quickly unstrung. Recurvature (*ta'jīr*) is the curving of the bow toward its back when unstrung, and is the opposite of incurvature (*inḥinā'*) which is the curving of the unstrung bow toward its belly so that it appears to the eye almost strung.[39] It should have more horn than wood because both the weight of the bow and its force depend upon the horn—the more horn it has, the stronger it is—although it is then more apt to become crooked in regions of unsuitable climatic conditions, while the more it has of wood and sinew, the straighter it remains, although its strength is then diminished. Therefore, one should strike a happy medium inclining toward the sparing use of horn.

The training or practice bow should be a little stronger than the capacity of the archer. After a little use it be-

another case, the highly recurved and very short fully composite bow. To analyze the citations, with their consequently conflicting measurements, is more than difficult and can be done only by appraisement of the context.

[39] These two words, *recurvature* and *incurvature*, are literal translations and have never been used previously in works on archery in the English language; the customary terms being *reflexion* and *following the string*. We will retain them, however, as they are convenient and seem to fit the requirements very well.

comes more manageable.[40] He should then increase its weight by adding to it one and a half dirhams of sinew. This operation should be repeated whenever the bow becomes too flexible and loses strength, until it has again reached the full limit of the archer's capacity.[41] Furthermore, the training bow should have wide arms, a rounded grip, and strong *siyahs*. Its sinew should exceed both its horn and its wood.

The target bow should be of moderate size and construction, with its wood less than its horn, and its sinew equal in thickness to its horn. Others have said that its component parts should be equal. The former opinion is, however, better. Furthermore, it should have a slender grip, while its arms should be recurved (*mu'ajjarah*) and moderate in size and width; the *siyahs* should, likewise, be moderate in length and recurvature. If these characteristics obtain, the target bow will be free of defects and its usefulness and accuracy will be increased.

The competition bow should have a rounded grip and long *siyahs*, and be recurved both in the grip and in the *siyahs*. Its arms should be narrow and rounded, with the lower less prominent than the upper, or, according to others, exactly the opposite, namely, the upper arm less prominent than the lower. Its horns should be of five or six

[40] This is the common experience of all archers and is due to two factors: one in the archer and the other in the bow. Naturally, the archer becomes stronger and more skillful with practice so that his bow feels lighter because of his own improvement. But the bow itself loses strength because of the compression and extension of its components; ligneous cells are crushed, sinews are stretched, and other forces of minute disintegration occur which, as a whole, lessen the power of the bow—a process technically known as *sinking*. Some archers who have shot composite bows tell us that they have found this sinking to be more rapid in such bows than in wooden ones, and our limited experience has bred in us the same opinion. It may be noted in passing that bows of steel undergo no demonstrable change.

[41] This passage is of great importance as proving that the Asiatics were able to restore or increase the cast of their bows by adding sinew to the back whenever it became convenient to do so. This fact, we think, has not been brought out in any other book that has been published in the English language.

pieces[42] and the width of two fingers shorter than the arrow—while the width of one finger may be added to the length of each *siyah*, which is equivalent to half the decrease in the length of the two arms. The longer and more dominant the *siyahs* and grip are, the faster and harder the arrow goes; while the looser the bow, the weaker it is and the safer from possible defects and flaws.

The weight in hand of the finished competition bow should be between twelve and fifteen *uqīyahs* [troy ounces of 480 grains], and the lighter in hand it is [i.e., the less its own heft], the faster and better is the flight of its arrow. Its string is always thin.[43]

The bow for trick shooting, according to some archers, should be like that of the Persians, with a square grip of moderate size, short and thick *siyahs* of almost equal length, and arms, likewise, of almost equal length and width. Furthermore it should be very flexible: in weight not more than half the capacity of the archer. In the judgment of the author this statement is correct, except for that part which says that the arms and *siyahs* of such a bow should be almost equal in length, respectively, as they are

[42] See Appendix, 9. Horns Used in Bows.

[43] This picture of the Oriental flight bow, which the author calls "the competition bow," fits perfectly into all known requirements. Because a short object which is bent will return to normal sooner than a long one of the same material, each bending arm of the bow is shortened by the breadth of two fingers. It is also rounded to provide depth and reduce wind resistance. To bring the bow up to the length necessary for the arrow, the grip and *siyahs* are made longer. Since the *siyahs* are inflexible and their movement is imparted by the arms, their greater length gives longer arcs for the nocks to travel. As these arcs are traversed almost as quickly as shorter ones would be, greater speed is given to the tightening of the string, on which the projection of the missile depends.

To understand the phrase "the looser the bow," one must remember that an unstrung Oriental bow may be so recurved that its ends may touch and make it form the letter O; or it may be even more recurved until the *siyahs* overlap and make it look like a pretzel. Obviously, when this recurvature has been reduced by stringing, and thus brought to a condition of incurvature, the internal tension, or potential force of the bow, is much greater than it would be if there had been little or no recurvature. Therefore, the bow with little recurvature would be less taut, or "looser" and "safer from possible defects."

in Persian bows; for it must be remembered that the center of the bow, according to the catholic consent of expert archers, is at a point the width of a finger from the top of the grip.

All of the details which we have mentioned concerning the construction of this composite bow are the result of long experience by master archers, all of whom are in agreement. Persian archers, however, have disagreed with them completely and said that the bow should be of symmetrical construction with both arms equal in size and both *siyahs* also equal, thereby making the central point of the bow at the middle of the grip. Some experts among the Persians, however, have maintained that the upper arm and the upper *siyah* should be slightly longer than the lower ones so that the center of the bow will fall at the two thirds point of its grip; that the arms should be wide and long, and that the sinew should constitute the smallest proportion in the construction of its parts. They claim that a bow so made will give a faster, harder, and more deadly arrow.

In the judgment of the author the claim of the Persian archers is decidedly wrong because, if the arrow leaves the bow at a point other than the central, it will be pushed by the bow in two different ways at the same time: with force by the shorter limb of the bow and with weakness by the long limb, with the result that it will wobble along its flight, and consequently its cast will be diminished and its accuracy decreased. It will not hit the mark, unless by accident. This may not be apparent to the eye but, if the disparity between the two limbs be accentuated, the wobbling will become noticeable.

The correct thing is what we have already quoted on the authority of the experts; namely, that the center of the bow should be at a point on the grip the width of one finger from its top, and that the upper arm of the bow together with its *siyah* constitute half of the entire bow, while the remaining part of the grip together with the lower arm and *siyah* comprise the other half of the bow. Consequently, the arrow passes at the middle of the bow which is the *kabid*; balance will then be obtained and the shooting will be accurate.

We have already mentioned that every individual has his own particular bow which is proportioned to his stature, and we shall soon show that every individual has his own particular arrow, also proportioned to his stature. This is based on a definite principle: the length of the bow is in direct proportion to the length of the arrow, and the length of the arrow is, in turn, in direct proportion to the size of the archer. The first we have already discussed; the second will be treated later.

It should be known that all the basic rules and principles which the experts and master archers, as a result of their long experience, have laid down concerning this science are completely unknown to the archers of our time. What now prevails and is known among our archers is the Persian system of archery which we have received from them, since the Damascene bows, which are at present the best and most perfectly constructed, as well as other bows now in use, are fashioned after the Persian bow in that their center lies at the two thirds point of the grip, or in the middle thereof, while the arms are of equal, or almost equal, length, and the *siyahs*, likewise, are of equal length or nearly so. Furthermore, the sinew constitutes the least of the component parts and the horn constitutes the greatest. Consequently, they are easily warped in this land of ours on account of the intense heat. For that reason it is almost impossible to find in the whole of Morocco a Damascene bow that is not warped.[44] Likewise, you can hardly

[44] This is an important paragraph. It takes us into the personal confidence of the author and shows us what he was: a true toxophilite who stood almost alone in his effort to revive this nearly forgotten but intrinsically fascinating art. It also furnishes the evidence which proves that he was a Moroccan writing in Morocco.

find a single arrow which fulfills the necessary and established requirements of construction or even a single archer who has a fair knowledge of the basic rules of archery.

Shooting, itself, in our days, is in a state of deterioration, far from abiding by the principles of experts. Consequently, it has become feeble and weak—lacking in force and accuracy—with the result that partisans of the foot bow and persons who are not familiar with the hand bow regard the latter as deficient in power and incapable of accurate aim. No intelligent man who understands the science of archery can tolerate such drivel. Has not God himself said in the Holy Koran: "Make ready against them what force ye can"? And has not the Apostle of God interpreted it as the Arab bow? "Say! Who knoweth best: ye or God?" Verily God is omniscient.

The best bows are those the horn of which is made of four to six pieces, or a little more or less, and the glue of which is plentiful, since the more glue the bow has, the harder it becomes, the more strongly its arrow travels, and the better it is in every respect; in fact, the quality of the bow depends on the glue. The more horn the bow contains, the more easily it is warped; while the more wood it contains, the straighter it will remain, although—with the greater proportion of wood—its arrow will fly with less force and it will become incurved more quickly, so that it may often seem to be strung while it is really unstrung. It is therefore advisable to strike a happy medium, using horn rather sparingly—a little more than wood—in order to avoid the flaws and defects already mentioned. This middle course will insure a strong and lasting bow since those characteristics, as well as a long and forceful cast of the arrow, result from a preponderance of the horn over the wood; whereas incurvation, weakness, and ineffectiveness of the bow result from preponderance of the wood over the horn.

XXXIII. On strings; how to make them and how to form their eyes

STRINGS should be carefully made so that they will not stretch in cold weather nor shrink in a warm climate.[45]

They are made of hide, of which the best is that of a lean camel, since such strings, if they are well made, are suitable for all seasons: cold, hot, or otherwise. In case no hide of a lean camel is available, that of a wild ass will do; and in the absence of wild ass hide, that of goats may be used. Goat hide, however, is good only in warm climates and is useless in cold and humid weather since it will then stretch because of dampness.

Strings may also be made of good silk or sinew, both of which are suitable for cold and humid climates but are useless in warm places because they swell up with the heat. Nor are strings made of silk or sinew good for very strong bows. They were, however, used by all the Slavs. Strings may also be made of bamboo, the use of which was current among all the Nubians as well as among many Persians. It is claimed that such strings are very good because they are not affected by climatic changes, though the material is rather brittle and offers the bow little help.[46] Strings may also be made of intestines, the product of which is known

[45] Bearing in mind the climate of Morocco (winter is the rainy season and summer the dry season), it is apparent that most of the effects which the author attributes to cold and heat are really due to the presence or absence of moisture. When uninfluenced by humidity, cold will slightly contract a string and heat expand it, but neither will be enough to be noticed by the archer. Portions of the text sufficiently indicate the author's real meaning.

[46] We have seen strings on African bows of the primitive tribes which consist of a single strip of bamboo. They are perhaps as much as a quarter of an inch in width but much less than that in thickness, being decidedly flat instead of round. The arrow for such a string has a flat heel, instead of a nock, and is held against the broad side by pressure between the thumb and forefinger. This pinch-hold gives a weak tractive power which would not suffice for a Persian bow, and so it is more than doubtful if the author had a string of that kind in mind. Bamboo is a grass and can be shredded. Possibly, strings of the regular type were made from its fibers, though we have never seen any nor have we read of them elsewhere.

as gut string and is good in warm weather only. Cold and damp weather makes them stretch. The best strings, however, are those made of hide since they are good for all kinds of bows, especially those that are hard to draw and are strong of cast.

To make a string, take the hide of a lean camel which has gone hungry through the winter and, therefore, has become emaciated and has not had an opportunity to become fattened at the coming of the spring. The younger the camel, the better is its hide. Soak it in cold water, avoiding completely the use of salt. Then cut it into three sections: the sides making two sections, and the back one. Hang the back section from a piece of wood, weigh it down, and—taking hold of it—scrape it with a sharp metal blade until it is thoroughly cleaned of all flesh. Then cut it in strips twice as wide as the finished string is to be, except that where the hide seems too thin it should be cut a bit wider, and where it is too thick, a bit narrower; because, if it be cut evenly, the thick parts will turn out to be too coarse in the finished product and the thin parts too fine—both of which are serious flaws. Therefore, be careful to cut it out as we have directed, so that the finished string may be even and uniform in thickness. The same operation should be followed with the side sections except that in this case the strips should be cut two and a half times as wide as the finished string.

The string should be coarse in three places; namely, the part whereon the arrow is nocked and the parts which make its two eyes. The strips should then be taken into a dark room where no air penetrates and hung from nails fixed along a board on one of the walls. In the loose end of each strip you cut a hole and insert into it a small piece of wood; then—taking the wood in one hand—start to twist it carefully and attentively, and, at the same time, stretch it out while rubbing it with something rough held in the other hand. When it has been sufficiently twisted and rubbed, weigh it down—the heavier the weight attached to it the better—until it is stretched out to its full limit, and leave it like that for several days until it is completely dry. Then remove and use.

While the hide is still wet, you may make the string by forcing the strip through a small iron ring attached to a strong handle. When making the string by this method, the hide should be cut in strips as wide as the ring itself. After pushing one end of the strip into the eye of the ring, insert into the eye a little piece of wood that is big enough to fill it out, support it with one hand and, with the other, hold the end of the strip and pull at it so as to force the strip through the ring. It will come through cleaned of all flesh and hair. You then finish it in the same manner as the first.

If you do not want it to stretch in the damp winter nor shrink in the dry summer, make an eye in either end, string it on a strong bow, and, while thus braced, soak it in water until it becomes soft. Then draw the bow several times until the string stretches out to its limit, at which time you unstring the bow, twist the string once, and brace the bow again—leaving it so until the string is dry. You then remove the string and fit it on another bow that is a little stronger, and soak it again in water until it stretches out fully; at which time you unstring the bow, give the string another twist, and brace it again on the same bow until it dries. The operation is repeated until the string ceases to stretch any more. It is then rubbed down carefully with a fine polishing stone, after which it should be given—in the summer—a coat of a thick solution of gum Arabic to protect it against shrinking because of the dry heat. Such protection will keep it strong as well as give it greater force for driving the arrow. In winter it should be rubbed with a fine polishing stone; then treated with a mixture of fox fat and yellow beeswax melted together, making sure that the string is warm before the mixture is applied. The way to warm the string is to rub it between two very smooth

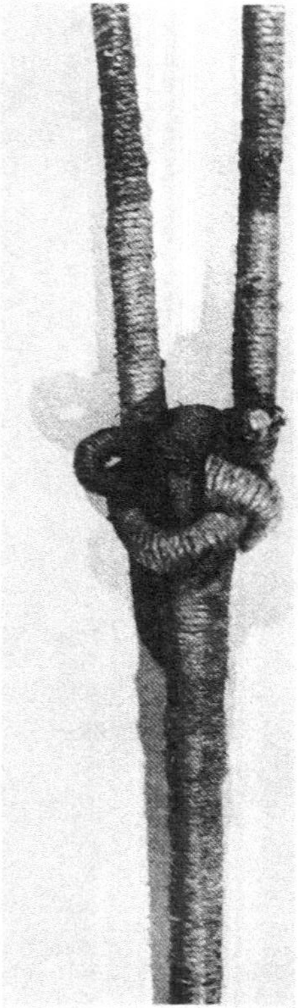

Genuine Bowstring Knot in a Chinese String

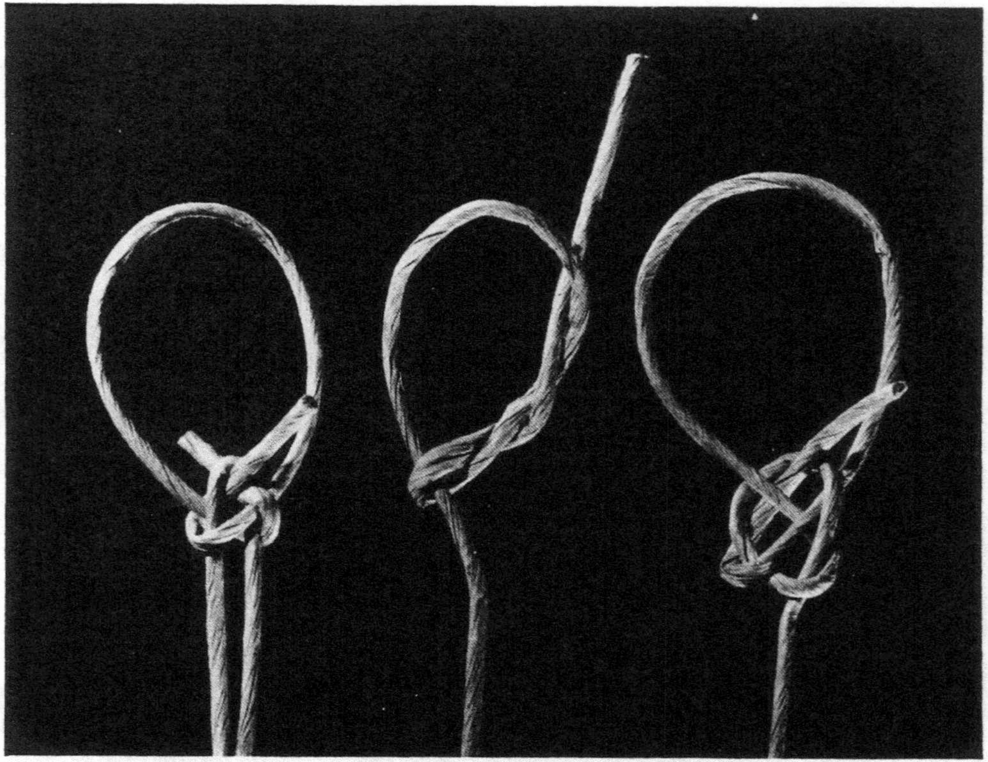

Asiatic Bowstring Knot, probably Khurasanian

Timber Hitch

Single Strand Bowstring Knot, possibly *Ṣa'dīyah*

stones. The mixture is thus thoroughly absorbed into the texture of the string which it renders waterproof and fit for using in the rain without damage.

There are three ways of making the eyes of a string.[47] The first is the so-called Turkish, which is good for coarse strings to be used with weak bows because of the ease with which it is undone. The second is the Khurasanian, which is the best and finest of all knots. The third is known as the *Ṣaʻdīyah*,[48] and is likewise good.

When using a string, have the thicker part up and the thinner part down. Some reverse this process and place the thinner part up and the thicker part down; but the first method is the better one since the strength of the bow lies in the upper limb, and upon it mainly depends the driving force of the bow. Therefore, the thicker part of the string should be on the side of the upper limb.

If the string be made of two pieces, have the point where the two pieces are joined together lie within the lower limb. If it be made with two connections, that is, of three pieces, have the shortest piece down and the longest piece up. If, when shooting with such a string, the arrow should wobble and wag in its flight, reverse the string, placing the shortest piece up. The arrow will then go straight because the knots are no longer opposite to each other [that is, in relation to their positions on the limbs].

When you make the eyes of the string, be sure that you use the same kind of knot in both, whether Turkish, Khurasanian, or *Ṣaʻdīyah*. Never mix them up, having a Khurasanian on one end and a Turkish or *Ṣaʻdīyah* on the other, lest you corrupt the quality of your shooting. Should the string stretch, for some reason, give it a twist or two and tie a knot in it just beside the eye (but never below it).

The eyes of the string are usually small in size. They

[47] See Appendix, 10. Knots.

[48] This Arabic adjective is derived from Ṣaʻdah, a small town near the fringe of the western Arabian desert.

should never be made large lest that militate against the shooting, increase its faults, and weaken the driving force of the bow—besides, oftentimes causing the string to slip off the nocks. The author of *The Book on the Different Kinds of Weapons* (*Kitāb Ajnās al-Silāḥ*) said that the eyes which incline toward being wide and long give greater driving force for the arrow, longer range, and harder hitting, although, he added, the arrow is apt to wobble in its flight and the string hit the forearm of the archer. Therefore, he who desires great driving force and long range should make the eyes of the string long and wide, ignoring the wobbling of the arrow, since he is after distance not accuracy. The present author is of the opinion that this statement is not plausible since the wobbling of an arrow in flight dissipates its force and reduces its range. Likewise, one eye should not be wide and the other narrow except so far as is necessitated by thickness of the upper part of the string and thinness of the lower.

XXXIV. On the length and shortness of the string

What is meant here by the length and shortness of the string is the distance between it and the grip when the bow is strung, not its length or shortness as measured from one end to the other. This is, as it were, a nomenclature in reverse, since when the distance between the string and the grip is large it is termed long, and when the distance between them is small it is called short, though, when measured from one end to the other, the string which is termed short is, in reality, longer than that which is termed long.[49]

[49] This naming "in reverse" is very unfortunate, as it is annoying and confusing—apparently not only to the reader but to the author himself, since he is not consistent throughout his manuscript but, in many places, uses the words *short* and *long* to indicate the actual measure of strings

The space between the string and the grip of a braced bow, the *siyahs* of which are short or of medium size, should not exceed a single span; while the space between the string and the grip of a braced bow with long *siyahs* should not be less than half a span.

The span (*shibr*) and half span (*fitr*) should be those of the owner of the bow himself, and not an average span nor average half span, because a tall archer whose hands are large requires a long arrow and, therefore, a long bow, in accordance with the principle which we have already laid down—namely, of the relations between the size of the individual archer and the arrow he uses, and between the arrow and the bow. The average span or half span, therefore, will not do; for it should be remembered that to every individual archer there is a bow proportionate to his size, as we shall soon discuss, as well as a string proportionate to his bow, as has already been treated of. We shall treat later of the thinness and thickness as well as the lightness and weight of the string in relation to the bow.

There are good and bad aspects of the long [i.e. high braced] string: praiseworthy and blameworthy. It is praiseworthy in so far as it increases the flight and force of the arrow, and enhances its power and penetration. The author, however, is of the opinion that this is, in reality, a blemish rather than an asset since it militates against the efficient performance of the bow; for the secret of the strength of the bow, the speed of its arrow, and the deadliness thereof, lies in the fact that its horn exceeds its wood so that when it is unbraced it recurves. You thus see that the carefully made bow which springs back and recurves whenever it is unbraced (even when used by an expert who handles it skillfully, fulfills all the prerequisite details, and never violates the principles laid down by the masters) will, because of the excessive length of its *siyahs*,

from end to end. In English, the distance between the string and the grip is called the *height of the string.*

gradually lose its recurvature and its property of springing back, until finally it acquires the property of incurvation and seems like one braced when it is actually unbraced. Thus, if you fit a bow with a long string and brace it, incurvation will soon appear in its belly; though, but for the long string, it would not appear unless after a protracted and arduous period of use.[50] It is the long string which causes recurvature to be transformed into incurvature and strength into weakness.

The blameworthy aspects of the long string include its tendency to slap against the forearm of the archer and to twist the neck of the bow, thereby disarranging the string and speeding the process of incurvation.

There are, likewise, good and bad aspects of the short string. Among the praiseworthy is that the bow is guarded against the quick development of incurvation in its belly and its neck is kept from being twisted, with consequent disarrangement of the string. Furthermore, the archer is safeguarded by the use of a short string against its slapping his forearm, and so is aided in his aim and accuracy.

The blameworthy aspects include its weakening effect on the strength of the arrow and on the shortening of its range.

The correct procedure, therefore, is to follow the instructions which we have already given.[51]

[50] This sudden blaming of long *siyahs* for producing incurvation of the bow seems to be an indirect way of saying that the string is too short—in actual length—for them—as long *siyahs* would have no such effect if the string were in proportion.

[51] The accuracy of two of the author's statements are open to dispute. At least in the American and English style of shooting—where the bow is of wood and the arrow passes on its left side—the forearm is much more likely to be hit by a low string than by a high one; and, also, a low string will cast an arrow farther than one of high bracing. Both of these facts are opposed to the sense of the text and it is hard to believe that the right sided shooting of a composite bow would cause widely different results.

XXXV. On the thinness and thickness of the string and on how to choose the correct and appropriate size

SOME archers, for instance the Egyptians, have favored the use of a thin and hard string, maintaining that it is better suited for casting the arrow, less visible on the bow, and more telling against the enemy. They were guided in their choice by the fact that the strings used in competitive archery [flight-shooting] are always thin, with all archers agreeing on this specification.

Others (namely, all the Persians) have preferred thick and coarse strings, asserting that they are better in every way. Ṭāhir al-Balkhi once said that he had examined a bow belonging to a certain Persian against the arrow of which none could protect himself because of its force and penetration, and found out that the bow was as flexible as those in current use, but that its string was coarse and as thick as a finger and that the metal head of its arrow was very large. He, therefore, made himself one exactly like it and tested it; only to find it very good. A certain archer stated that the coarse string is better for the bow: more penetrating, more easily drawn, and superior to the thin in warfare and target shooting; while the thin string is better for competitive shooting and for shooting at distant marks. Ṭāhir declared that the thick string is more deadly at short distances and the thin is more telling at long distances.

The thinness and thickness of the string, as well as its relatively appropriate size, are determined by bracing its bow, drawing the string with the thumb and index finger the length of one and a half spans, quickly releasing it and listening to its twang. If the twang is sharp and high, the string is too thin for the bow; if it is moderate in sharpness and lowness, the string is just right; if it is low, the string is too thick.

XXXVI. On the weight of the string in relation to the weight of the bow

WHEN the bow weighs seventy rotls, its appropriate string should weigh three or three and a half dirhams; when its weight is sixty rotls, the string should weigh two or two and a half dirhams; when its weight is thirty rotls, the string should weigh one or one and a half dirhams. All these specifications are according to the Khurasanian school.

Others among the Persians maintain that when the bow weighs one hundred and fifty rotls, the string should weigh four dirhams; when it weighs eighty rotls, the string should weigh three dirhams; when it weighs seventy rotls, the string should, likewise, weigh three dirhams.

Some archers have maintained that when the bow weighs seventy rotls, the string should weigh from three or three and a half to four dirhams. The same thing is true when the bow weighs eighty or ninety rotls. When the bow weighs one hundred rotls, the string should weigh four and a half dirhams; when it weighs one hundred and fifty rotls, the string should weigh from four and a half to five dirhams; when it weighs two hundred rotls, the string should weigh from five or six to eight dirhams. This we have tried ourselves and found to be good.

In the case of the string of the competition bow: when the bow weighs one hundred rotls, the string should weigh from two to three dirhams; if the bow weighs less, the decrease in the weight of the string should be proportional.[52]

[52] See Appendix, 11. The Dirham and Its Equivalents.

XXXVII. On the names of the various kinds of arrows and their different parts; and on the length of each kind, the desirable wood from which to make it, and the manner of its paring

BEFORE a shaft is fletched it is called featherless (*qidḥ*); after it is fletched it is called feathered (*murayyash*); and after the head has been added it is called an arrow (*sahm*). The notch cut into it for the string is called the nock (*fūq* or *kazz*); the two cusps (sing. *sharkh*) of the nock are called the two branches, or edges, or sides. The sinew whipped around the base of the nock is called the ring (*uṭrah*). The part where the feathers are fixed is called the scraped place (*ḥafw*); while the part next to it is called the breast [literally—the copious portion, *wāfirah*]. The part next to the breast is called the body, or trunk, or stem (*matn*), and is the tapered portion up to the arrowhead. The sinew whipped around the end of the shaft for the purpose of securing the arrowhead is called the ligament (*raṣfah* or *raṣafah*). The place where the arrowhead is inserted into the shaft is called the socket (*ruʿẓ*); and the arrowhead is the metal point [literally—iron, *ḥadīd*] of the arrow, no matter what shape it may be; while the extreme point (*ẓubah*) of the arrowhead together with its corners constitute its edge.

The *mirrīkh* [literally—a flexible branch] is a long arrow with four feathers; while the *ḥaẓwah* [literally—a small rod] is a little arrow called by the professionals *ḥusbān* [literally—a hailstone] or *dawdan* and is shot in the groove of a reed or cane. The *rahb* [literally—emaciated] is an enormous arrow with a large arrowhead.

Great disagreement exists among experts concerning the length of an arrow. Abu-Hāshim maintained that the length of an arrow should equal one cubit, measured against the archer's own arm, plus the length of his forearm; or the length of his own leg and foot, or leg and forearm; or the length of his forearm plus the width of his chest. Ṭāhir, on the other hand, maintained that the length of an arrow should equal the distance between the base of the armpit and the extreme tip of the middle finger. Isḥāq held that it should be equal to the extent of one's ability to draw fully with ease and grace.

Others advocated the length of eight fists of the archer's own hand, others said nine, others ten, others eleven, and others twelve. Still others maintained that it should equal the distance between the outer ends of the horns of the archer's bow when the bow is strung, while others said when the bow was unstrung. I hold that all these theories and views are worthless except that of Isḥāq, the principle which he laid down as being the most reasonable and correct. It is the one that should be followed.[53]

The best kind of wood is that which combines in itself hardness and lightness as well as even texture and smooth surface. It should be strong—not loose, nor swollen, nor thin—and be such as would split lengthwise and not breadthwise; since when it breaks breadthwise it means that the wood is thin and slender, as well as weak, loose, light, and dry; while when it breaks lengthwise it means that the wood is hard, rich, and strong. The best wood in the East is *shawḥaṭ*,[54] which is the same as *khalanj*, and

[53] See Appendix, 12. Lengths of Arrows.

[54] It is this reference to *shawḥaṭ* that rouses our doubts as to its restricted identity with yew, for yew is too crooked and heavy to make the best arrows and, in most localities, is also too rare and expensive. Some of the highest authorities on wood in the Smithsonian Institution and in various national and state departments of forestry are also interested in archery, yet none of those whom we have consulted can find a proven definition for *shawḥaṭ*. When the author of the manuscript uses the word to name the wood that is most suitable for bows, we believe that he means it to indicate yew. When he uses it for arrows we feel, but cannot prove, that he refers to some sort of pine, cedar, or spruce that is like yew. *Shawḥaṭ* may be a somewhat generic name which covers several related species, just as the English use the word "deal" for many kinds of resinous woods. This hypothesis is rendered more plausible because of the fact that *shawḥaṭ* is stated to be synonymous with *nab'*, *shiryān*, and *khalanj*.

in Andalusia the best wood is red pine which has become dry and light. The older it is, the better.

Arrows made of some kinds of wood are heavy and travel slowly when shot, while others are light and travel fast. To find out which is which, take the sawdust of several woods and place them separately in water; the one which moves the slowest in water is the one which travels fastest when shot.

Another way to determine which wood is the more suitable is to take two billets and split from each one an arrow stave which you will trim, force through a ring to obtain uniformity of size, and then balance against the other on scales. The one which is lighter is the one you should use. You will then—after having trimmed them and forced them through the ring—fletch them with feathers which weigh exactly the same, fix on them arrowheads which are also of equal weight, and then shoot with each. The one which travels faster is the one you should use.

All this pertains to the arrows of competitive shooting. In shooting for other than competitive purposes, however, a heavy arrow is sometimes better than a light one, as we shall describe later—particularly in shooting at a ring or a hair, and in other such stunts of trick shooting.

The best time for cutting the wood for arrows, as well as for anything else, is during the autumn season when the leaves have fallen off the trees and the dampness of the branches has diminished. The wood should also be hung in a house wherein a fire is lit, so that the heat of the fire may remove the remaining dampness of the wood until it is completely dry. It should then be left hanging for at least two months.

The making and shaping of arrows may follow one of three modes: the first [or barreled] arrow is thick at the upper trunk like a snake; the second [or cylindrical] arrow is even throughout the whole length of the shaft; the third [or tapered] arrow is thick at one end and gradually becomes thinner down to the other end, like the tail of a mouse.

The barreled arrow [*muṣaddar*—literally: broad-breasted] is of two kinds. One has the first third of the arrow thin, the second third thick, and the final third terminating with the nock thin like the first. This kind is used by the Egyptians and by many in the East, and is by far the best kind of arrow. The second kind of barreled arrow has one half of the shaft thin and the other half thick up to the place of the feathers, where it becomes thin again.

The cylindrical arrow, of even thickness, is shaved down uniformly, being of the same size from its head to the place of the feathers, where it becomes thin. In this connection we might say that all archers are agreed concerning the fact that the place of the feathers should be thin in all kinds of arrows.

The tapered arrow, which resembles the tail of a mouse, is thick at the fore end and gradually becomes thinner and thinner down to the place of the feathers, where it becomes thinner still.

Thin and light arrows are more penetrating and faster in their flight, while thick and heavy arrows offer greater accuracy in hitting the mark.

The correct method of fashioning arrows is shaving along the grain of the wood and never turning in a lathe, because turning in a lathe enters the arrow broadwise and cuts its straight grain and does away with its strength and opens its pores so that air enters into it when it is shot and spoils its course, dissipates its strength, and makes it wobble in flight. Therefore the correct method of fashioning it is by shaving and no other should be used.

Among the things which should be known and by all means remembered in connection with the making of arrows is that the beginning of the arrow where the head is should be toward the root of the tree and the arrowhead should be inserted in that end, while the nock where the string is should be cut in the end of the stave which has been nearest in the tree to where the leaves grow. This is a principle which has been forgotten by many an archer. Some are completely ignorant of it; others are aware of it but have ignored it and chosen not to bother themselves with it. It is one of the secrets of the art. Another is paring the arrow rather than turning it.

Even when you cannot readily tell which end is the base of the branch and which end is the upper part where the leaves grow, you can determine which is which by shaving the branch evenly throughout and placing it in a vessel of water. The end which tips down in water is the base of the branch where the arrowhead should be inserted.

Another way to determine which end of the branch is its base is to take the branch and shave it evenly throughout as has been mentioned already, find out by careful measurement its middle point, mark it, and then lift the branch with your hand from this middle point. The end which tips down is the base wherein the arrowhead should be inserted.

XXXVIII. On arrowheads; the different kinds, their various uses, how to fix them on the shaft; and the manner of cutting arrow-nocks

THE different kinds of arrowheads are numerous but fall under five basic shapes: those which, in cross section, are triangular, square, or round; and those which, in general shape, are elongated or caplike.

The triangular are of two sorts: long and short. The very short kind is suitable for the penetration of shields and other metal armor except iron helmets, and the like, on which an arrow would be likely to slip. The long triangular arrowheads are suitable for shooting against metal helmets and other things on which an arrow would be likely to slip. They are also good for the penetration of all varieties of wood. The appropriate shafts for these triangular arrowheads are the cylindrical in which the end of the shaft should be a little thinner than the triangulation of the arrowhead. There is a third kind of triangular arrowhead which has a triangular tip and flat edges and is good for every purpose.

Square-shaped arrowheads are also of two varieties: long and short. The long kind is furnished with four extended barbs and is suitable for shooting at an enemy whose body is not shielded with any armor, as well as for hunting down beasts of prey such as lions and the like. When this weapon enters the body of the victim it cannot be withdrawn since the barbs cling to the flesh within.

The short and compact square-headed arrowhead is suitable for shooting against shields, breastplates, and coats of armor.

Round-shaped arrowheads are, likewise, of two varieties: long and short. The short are particularly suitable for the penetration of shields, while the long are good for penetrating coats of armor and breastplates as well as wood and the like.

Elongated arrowheads are of three varieties: short, long, and barbed. All have hollow, cylindrical bases into which the shafts of the arrows are inserted. The short have wide, sharp edges like Byzantine spears, and a sharp barb on either side. They are suitable for shooting down enemies without armor and beasts of prey. The long are usually about four fingers in length, with long edges and thick cylindrical bases into which the shafts of the arrows are inserted as we have already mentioned. They are suitable for hunting down strong beasts of prey, like lions, and animals which quickly flee, like deer. The barbed have short edges from which very sharp barbs protrude. They are suitable for shooting against enemies without armor and beasts of prey.

The simple caplike arrowheads are like spearheads, with all their variations, and have hollow bases into which the shafts are inserted, just like the spears.

The manner of fixing the arrowhead onto the shaft consists of boring a hole a trifle shorter than the tail of the arrowhead in the place where the arrowhead should be inserted, placing the tail therein, fitting the head with a guard (*'atīq*), and then pressing with the palm against the guard until the tail reaches the limit of the hole. You then remove the guard and hammer with a mallet against the other end of the shaft opposite the hole until the entire tail is lodged in the hole. The guard consists of a small piece of metal, square in shape, into which a cavity is bored in the form of a particular arrowhead: triangular, square, or round, or whatever the case may be. The cavity should be quite deep but a little narrower than the tail itself so that the latter may be held firmly without causing its point to be flattened or injured. Then the part surrounding the hole should be reinforced by whipping it with sinew.

An archer desiring a more perfect job may, after boring the hole as we have already described, split the end of the shaft carefully in three places in order to facilitate the insertion of the tail of the arrowhead, fill the hole with thick glue, insert the tail to the limit, and then strap it very hard with a strong thread made of hair until it dries up completely. Then file down and whip with sinew. It is also good to leave a little of the wood particles in the hole because they strengthen the glue around the metal of the arrowhead. This is all concerning the fitting of arrowheads with solid tails.

Those with sockets are fitted in the same way as spears

are fitted and are no good because they tend to break the arrow shaft. They may be used only against an enemy without armor and in hunting, where the archer does not mind having his arrows break.

In shooting against hard surfaces, such as shields and the like, nothing should be used except arrows with solid tails.

The slot of the nock, which is the notch where the string rests, is of two kinds: one with long cusps and one with short. Those who advocate the long cusps maintain that the arrow rests more firmly on the string therewith, while those who prefer the short cusps hold that the arrow emerges more quickly in its flight from the string. The best nock, however, is that which is neither too large nor too small, neither too wide nor too narrow.

XXXIX. On feathers and fletching

THE feathers of an arrow are known as vanes (*qudhadh*). The best feathers are those of the eagle, next those of the vulture, then those of the falcon and the like, and then those of the sea birds. In the absence of feathers, paper may be used. The feathers of the tail are better than the feathers of the wings because the latter are not as even and straight. The small feathers of the wing are still better than the feathers of the tail because they are softer. Some maintain that the feathers of the right wing give the arrow a greater velocity, while others hold that the feathers of the left wing offer greater speed. In any case, when the feathers of the right wing are used be sure to aim at the left side of the target; and when the feathers of the left wing are employed be sure to focus your aim at the right side of the mark.

Feathers should be straight, moderate in size and weight

and in length and width, and, above all, no single feather should weigh more than the other nor be placed higher or lower than the other, lest the arrow wobble in its flight. The best results are obtained by taking the central part of the feather and discarding the ends.

Every feather has a back and a belly. When you fix the feathers onto the shaft be sure that they are back to belly in position. When the feathers are back to belly on the shaft they are described as *lu'ām*, and such arrangement is the best; no other should be used. When the feathers are arranged back to back or belly to belly, the result is poor and undesirable. Such arrangement is described as *lughāb* [literally: weak] and should never be used. When fixing the feathers to the shaft be sure that they are opposite the sides of the arrowhead, each feather facing one side. To fix them otherwise is wrong and will militate against the accuracy of your shooting.

The rule for the number of feathers is four, and upon this all the Persians agreed. It is the best preferred among them and they claim that "feathers are the messengers of death"; and that four messengers are better than three. The people of Khurasan, however, have favored the use of three feathers, substituting for the fourth by pushing with the lower part of the wrist. Some of the clever experts of this profession have favored the use of six feathers: three large and three small in between the large.

A certain author on archery related that he had seen an expert trim his arrow with two side or flank feathers beside the nock and a third, known as the male (*dhakar*) feather, next to the arrowhead. He further said that he himself had tried it and found it to be good, preventing the arrow from turning or wobbling. The arrow falls on the target exactly as it had left the bow.

In short, too much feather slows the arrow and too little speeds its flight. However, while four feathers offer greater accuracy, with three feathers the length and speed of the flight is increased. The arrow has been likened to a ship; the feathers corresponding to the rudder with which the ship is steered. If the rudder is too heavy, it slows the ship down and may even cause it to sink; if it is too light, the ship will roll and pitch and be out of control. Experts have declared that this is an apt simile.

Experts have disagreed as to how far the feathers should be from the nock. Most Persians of Khurasan favor affixing them immediately next to the nock, and prefer them to be long, spiraled and high, except near the nock where they should be low. Advocates of the intermediate school in Khurasan favor having them five or six fingers removed from the nock and prefer them long and low.[55]

Experts, however, would limit the distance between the feathers and the nock to about the width of the fingers arranged for the count of one, and would rather have the feathers unspiraled. A certain archer said that, in his opinion, those who shoot "shower" arrows and engage in warfare should set the feathers far from the nock and have them spiraled; while those who shoot at close targets should set them as close to the nock as one fingerbreadth, or perhaps a little less. Feathers close to the nock offer greater accuracy, while those removed from it offer greater speed. The best spacing, however, is the width of the hand when the fingers are arranged for the count of one.

Most Persians prolong the feathers and claim that their length offers greater speed and longer range. The longest they use are six to seven fingers long. The experts of this

[55] This distance of five or six fingerbreadths from nock to feather is extraordinarily great and affords additional evidence of the fact that Arabian arrows were sometimes very long, as we deduced from the text on page 104. The greatest distance from nock to feather that we can find among our collection of exotic arrows is two and a quarter inches, occurring in Chinese war arrows that are thirty-eight inches in length, over all, and have twelve inch feathers. This is practically the same as the width of the three large fingers in "the count of one" (see page 112) that is mentioned below. Most arrows—everywhere—are fletched as close to the nock as will leave room for the fingers or the thumb and some Oriental arrows have no space there at all.

profession, however, prefer shortening the feathers, limiting them to four or five fingers in length; while for distant shooting they limit them to three fingers, claiming that the short feathers offer greater speed and longer range.

Other archers prefer to have the feathers low, claiming that low feathers offer greater speed and longer range; while others favor having them high, claiming that high feathers offer greater speed and longer range. Others, however, advocate the intermediate position and choose feathers of medium size.

Again, some archers prefer the use of the feathers of the right wing, holding that they offer greater speed and longer range; others favor the feathers of the left wing, claiming for them the same properties: greater speed and longer range; others would rather use the feathers of the tail, saying that they are best because they are flat and even as well as moderate in stiffness and softness; while others prefer the use of the small feathers of the wings.

Some archers trim the ends of the feathers close and leave the central part high. This method is followed by most of the Persians. Experts, however, leave the end toward the nock untrimmed and trim closely the end toward the arrowhead. This type of trimming is called the martin trim, because it is shaped like the wing of a martin.

XL. On the weight of arrows, arrowheads, and feathers

ARCHERS have disagreed violently concerning the weight of arrows, arrowheads, and feathers. Some have maintained that for a bow of twenty rotls an arrow of three dirhams should be had, and for a bow of thirty rotls an arrow of four dirhams. For every increase of ten rotls in the weight of the bow a corresponding increase of one dirham should be introduced into the weight of the arrow.

Others have said that the weight of the arrow should never be less than seven dirhams and never more than twenty dirhams no matter how stiff or how flexible the bow may be. If the bow is a flexible one and less than eighty rotls in weight, its arrow should be of seven dirhams, that is: six dirhams less one third of a dirham for the weight of the wood, one dirham for the weight of the arrowhead, and one third of a dirham for the weight of the glue and feathers.

If a bow is eighty rotls in weight, its arrow should weigh ten dirhams: eight and one half dirhams for the wood, and one and a half dirhams for the arrowhead, feathers, and glue. For bows above a hundred rotls in weight, the arrow should weigh from sixteen to twenty dirhams—never beyond that if you wish to insure accuracy and speed.

Ṭāhir al-Balkhi related, on the authority of his grandfather, Shāpūr dhu-'l-Aktāf [literally: Shāpūr of the shoulders; Shāpūr II, A.D. 310-379], that the weight of the arrow of a stiff bow should be twelve dirhams, ten of which belong to the shaft and two to the arrowhead and feathers. With such an arrow the kings of Persia were wont to shoot. They boasted of shooting light arrows with stiff bows. Ṭāhir said that, if the bow were thirty rotls in weight, the arrow should be eight and one third dirhams and the range one hundred cubits; if the bow were forty rotls in weight, the arrow should be the same—eight and one third dirhams—and the range one hundred and twenty-five cubits; if the bow were fifty rotls, the arrow should be the same—eight and one third dirhams—and the range one hundred and fifty cubits; if the bow were sixty rotls in weight, the arrow should be ten dirhams and the range one hundred and seventy cubits; likewise, if the bow were ninety rotls and the range two hundred cubits, the arrow should be ten dirhams; if the bow were one hundred rotls, the arrow should be from twelve to sixteen dirhams and the range from two hundred and seventy cubits to three hundred cubits. The weight of the arrow should not go beyond this and the range cannot be increased.

Some archers have maintained that target arrows should weigh from twelve to sixteen dirhams; never more for those who desire accuracy and speed. War arrows, however, should weigh from fifteen to twenty dirhams. This is, indeed, what we have tried and found good. The war arrow should have a large and wide metal arrowhead. Experts avoid using heavy arrows because of their many flaws and blemishes and because of their ineffectiveness. They would rather use light arrows with stiff bows as the arrows then travel straight without wobbling.

Others have said that arrows suitable for target shooting should be heavy and have abundant feathers. I, myself, used to shoot at the target with an arrow weighing over twenty dirhams.

It has been said that thin and fine arrows are suitable for distant targets and for enemies who are far away. Near targets, trick shooting and stunts, as well as small minute targets, require heavy arrows that are round in shape [cylindrical] and weigh about fifteen dirhams. Every archer should test himself with both varieties, the heavy and the light. In short, light arrows give greater penetration and longer range while heavy ones insure greater accuracy. For every kind of shooting, however, there is a particular weight of arrow.

The arrowhead, according to some archers, should weigh one seventh of the arrow, while the feathers should weigh one seventh of the arrowhead. Others have held that the arrowhead should weigh one eighth of the arrow and the feathers one eighth of the arrowhead. Still others have maintained that the arrowhead should equal one ninth of the arrow and the feathers one ninth of the arrowhead. If, therefore, the weight of the arrow were seven dirhams, the weight of the wood would be six dirhams less one seventh of a dirham, the arrowhead would be one dirham, and the feathers one seventh of a dirham.

When the second ratio prevails, the wood will be six dirhams and one eighth of a dirham, the arrowhead seven eighths of a dirham, and the feathers seven eighths of one eighth of a dirham. When the third ratio is followed, the wood will be six dirhams and one ninth of a dirham and one ninth of one ninth of a dirham, the arrowhead seven ninths of a dirham, and the feathers seven ninths of one ninth of a dirham.

The dirham used here is the so-called dirham of weight (*dirham al-kayl*). It is equivalent to fifty grains and two fifths of a grain of barley of medium size. Every eleven and one ninth dirhams of this legal weight make one *uqīyah*.[56] In terms of our large dirhams which are current in Morocco in the two-dirham unit, the legal dirham of weight is equivalent to three dirhams and one eighth of a dirham, approximately.

The reason for calling this dirham the dirham of weight (*dirham al-kayl*) is because it is the basis of the rotl (which equals twelve *uqīyahs*), the *mudd* (which equals six and one third rotls), and the *ṣā'* (which equals twenty-six and two thirds rotls). It is the legal dirham of Islam. It was described by abu-Muḥammad ibn-'Aṭīyah[57] in his treatise on weights and measures (*al-Makāyīl w-al-Awzān*).

[56] See Appendix, 13. Relative Weights.

[57] Ibn-'Aṭīyah was a distinguished scholar in Andalusia, Spain. He died *Anno Hegirae* 542, *Anno Domini* 1164.

XLI. On sundry points not yet mentioned concerning the competition bow, the description of its arrow, and the manner of its use, together with some of the tricks employed in competitions

WE HAVE already described the competition bow; there is no sense in repeating that. One thing, however, was left out which we shall now state; namely, that it should be made of *shawḥaṭ*, *nab'*, orange, or any similar wood which is light and flexible.[58] The wood should be felled at the right season (the autumn) and left to dry in the shade, thereby becoming a better absorbent of glue. The horn should be taken from goats and should be soaked in water for a long time. The string should be thin and strong, and in length almost that of the bow itself.[59]

The arrow of the bow of competition should be round, thin, spindle-shaped [barreled], light, hard, strong, and free from any weakness. It is thinned down excessively next to the nock and trimmed with pinion feathers. The feathers should be the width of three fingers in length and

[58] In a composite bow the central lamellar base need not necessarily be made of a variety of wood that would be suitable for self bows as the horn and sinew provide the real strength and the wood serves for little more than a frame for them to be glued to. So, if *nab'* should really be white poplar, as suggested in the footnote on page 9, it might do very well because of its power of holding glue. Perhaps the same could be said for orange. Excellent modern wooden bows have been made on a sort of composite principle; for example: with a hickory back, a dagame belly, and a central layer of practically inert beechwood.

[59] The length of the string, in this instance, is not that confusing "nomenclature in reverse" of Section XXXIV, where a "long" string was actually a short one, but it really means what it says. Therefore, since the string is long, it would not bend the bow very much in the bracing. The bow is then called "low-braced" and the height of the string from the grip is short. Both empirical and mathematical tests have proved that a bow will cast further when it is low-braced than when it is braced too high, although there is naturally a definite minimum in effective low-bracing. Here the author seems to recognize that fact and to express it quite casually, which is particularly interesting when we recall that on page 99 he made the directly contrary assertion that high-bracing "increases the flight and force of the arrow."

trimmed low on the end toward the nock and on the end toward the head. Another kind may be made like the wing of the martin. This is done by trimming each feather at its base and making its tip similar in shape to the tip of the wing of the martin. The tip of each feather should be toward the nock. The feathers should be three in number and placed at a distance from the nock.

The heads of these arrows should be light and made of iron or ivory, or of the quill of the feathers of an eagle.

Into the groove of the nock at its middle point, a hole, two thirds of a grain of barley in size, is sometimes bored with the point of an awl or some such instrument. It is supposed to enhance its speed, accelerate its flight, and strengthen its drive.

The arrow, including the arrowhead and the feathers, should weigh six dirhams; others said seven dirhams, and still others said eight dirhams. The author maintains that there is, in reality, no disagreement here, because the weight of the arrow depends on the stiffness or flexibility of the bow. Normally, competition bows should have light arrows; but, in many cases, even an arrow of eight dirhams is too light for a competition bow.

Furthermore, the arrows should be made by forcing them through a ring as has already been described under the section which treats of the making of arrows. Arrows for competition bows should be shorter than the ordinary arrows by the width of a fist. If the ordinary arrow measures the width of ten fists, the competition arrow should measure nine. Others held that it should be shorter than the ordinary arrow by only one degree—a degree being the width of one finger.

Finally the competition bow should be heavier than the ordinary bow by three rotls.

When you desire to compete, take your stand obliquely, and grip the bow with the Persian hold, which is the oblique hold. Place the thumb of your left hand between the index finger and the middle finger, project the lower tip of the bow a little away from your hip, and face the wind; but do not shoot skyward lest the wind force the arrow down and lessen its speed; likewise, do not shoot downward lest its range diminish. Lean on the right leg more than on the left, and look up; not to the place where you intend to shoot. Then draw quickly with one continuous draw, straighten your stand gradually as you draw, and then release with a sudden jerk without pause. Experts hold that in target shooting the pause is both desirable and good, whereas in competitive flight shooting it is very bad. Your release should therefore be quick and sudden without pause.

Some archers strike or pound with the right foot on the ground at the moment of release, while others do the same with the left, and still others do nothing of the sort. Indeed, everyone does what he has been accustomed to do. Some archer declared that in his opinion he whose left hand is stronger than his right should pound the ground with his right foot at the moment of release, while he whose right hand is stronger than the left should pound the ground with his left foot; and he whose hands are of equal strength should avoid pounding the ground with either foot. Furthermore, when one hand is stronger than the other, shooting is spoiled.[60]

[60] Many modern flight shooters actually do this pounding with the advanced foot—either by instinct or design—and it is interesting to observe that the impulse manifested itself just as strongly four centuries ago as it does today. At the moment of loosing, the flight shooter lunges forward and upward and stamps downward with his front foot to accentuate the attitude and preserve the balance of the body. Since the majority of archers are right-handed and the bow is held in the left hand, this advanced foot is normally the left one; but for him whose "left hand is stronger than his right"—the left-handed archer—the right hand holds the bow and the right foot is the one which does the stamping. Thus the anonymous "some archer" had a good deal of truth on his side. However, if he did have thoughts like these in mind, our author apparently misinterpreted them in the bias of his own conceptions: attributing the inequality of brachial strength not to right- or left-handedness—with the resulting contrast of posture—but to a lack of even tension between the arms during the drawing of the bow.

The best season for competitive shooting is autumn, the best region is the one least humid and damp, and the best time is at the two ends of the day: the early morning and the early evening, unless there be excessive dew or rain, in which case the middle of the day and the end thereof are best.

The best wind is in the north when it is not strong. You should shoot with the wind and not against it. Likewise, never shoot on days which are stormy, or excessively humid, or excessively windy, or extremely hot, because all of these conditions militate against the strength of the bow and decrease its range. Therefore, shoot under favorable climatic conditions and at the two ends of the day.

When two archers compete, using the same bow and the same arrow, the better archer wins. When they are equally skillful, the stronger archer wins. When they are of equal skill and strength, the one who shoots first wins, because the bow is always stiffer and stronger when first braced. It is, therefore, necessary that they shoot with two arrows each. The first archer shoots his first arrow and hands the bow over to the second archer who will, likewise, shoot his first arrow. Thereupon the bow is unbraced and left unstrung for about an hour until it regains its original strength and stiffness. Then it is braced and the second archer shoots his second arrow and hands the bow over to the first archer, who will then shoot his second arrow.

If they have only one arrow, the first archer begins, and, having shot the arrow, unbraces the bow and leaves it unstrung for a while until it regains its normal limit in stiffness and strength. He then should brace it again and shoot for the second time. The same should be done by the other competing archer.

Know, too, that the archer who uses an iron, or copper,

The assertion that neither foot should be pounded in the case of balance between "hands of equal strength," quite possibly may be the author's personal addition to the meaning of the authority whom he cites—a completion of the picture according to his own lights.

or silver, or gold thumb-tip will, all else being equal, outshoot the one who uses a leather thumb-tip. The one who uses a tight thumb-tip will outdo the other who uses too wide a tip. Likewise, he whose string has narrow and small eyes will outshoot the one whose string has large and wide eyes, since the wideness of the eyes of the string weakens the driving force of the bow. Such eyes, therefore, should be avoided. The author of the *Waṣf Ajnās al-Silāḥ* (Description of the Different Kinds of Weapons) maintained that wide eyes offer a greater driving force; but this is, indeed, not true and has been discussed in the section on strings. Similarly, the archer who uses a new string outdoes him who employs an old one or uses a string made of goat skin, because among the properties of goat skin are its softness and sogginess, both of which weaken the driving force of the bow. Finally, the archer who uses a string of good and finished workmanship outshoots him who employs one of faulty and crude manufacture; and he who employs a thin string outdoes him who uses a thick one.

Here follow some tricks not infrequently resorted to by competitors:

When two compete using the same arrow, and one of the two bores a small hole into the shaft next to the base of the nock and close to the feathers and then gives it to his opponent to shoot but, when he regains it in order to shoot his turn, stops the hole with wax, he will outshoot his opponent.

When one of two competitors secretly undoes the twist of the string at a certain point, wets it with saliva, and offers it to his opponent to shoot but then, on regaining it to shoot in his turn, unbraces the bow and restores the twist as well as dries the string by rubbing it with his sleeve and, after bracing the restored string, shoots, he will beat his opponent.[61]

[61] It is the very last, final jerk of the fully tightened string that sends the arrow off on its flight. If the fibers of the string are separated in some

If the feathers of the arrow are broad and, after one of the competitors has shot, the other trims the feathers a little and shoots in his turn, he will win.

If one of the competitors should wet one of the side feathers of the arrow, and hand it over to his opponent to shoot, and later, when his own turn comes, dry the wet feather with his sleeve and expose it to the wind to stiffen a bit, and then shoot it, he would win.

If two competitors have agreed to shoot the same arrow, and the one who gets hold of it first should—with an awl prepared for the purpose—bore a hole at the midpoint of the base of the nock where the string rests, and then should shoot, he would win. If he should shoot first with such an arrow and, just before handing it over to his competitor should stop the hole with wax, he would win.

All these tricks give an advantage to the archer who is aware of them and employs them secretly in his competitions, especially when his opponent is unfamiliar with them. But they are all despised except in wagers where the competitors have to use the same bow and the same arrow. Even in wagers they are considered unlawful since they are nothing but cheating. The only reason for enumerating them is to warn the unsuspecting and ignorant of their existence so that they may be on the lookout for them.

place and kept apart by spit, time and energy are lost when those fibers are pulled together again by the shot; and the sharp, efficient twang is lost from the bowstring just as surely as the clear tone of the string of a musical instrument is lost if it be similarly maltreated. In fact, the bow is the earliest form of stringed musical instrument, and many primitive races will use the same bow for shooting and making music. But—to return to the subject—the untwisted and ensalivated string will not shoot so far as one that has not been treated in this manner.

XLII. On thumb-tips and the various kinds thereof

A THUMB-TIP—which is called *kustubān* by the Persians and *khayta'ah* by the Arabs—consists of a ring of leather or some other material. It is worn over the right thumb, leaving the nail and knuckle exposed, and is used for the protection of the thumb against injuries which are usually caused by the string when it is drawn and released. Its use is necessary except when the archer employs a very weak bow for executing some stunt or for shooting at a near target. Shooting without a thumb-tip, whenever possible, is better and offers greater accuracy. For this reason [to resemble the bare skin], a thumb-tip should be made of leather that is even in texture and moderate in thickness, and should be lined with very fine leather and sewn with great care. An almost invisible groove should be made in it for the string. The end which lies on the tip of the thumb should be fashioned like a small, broad bean of moderate thickness; not so long as to impede the string, nor so short as to fail to protect the thumb from the action of the string. In width it should be the same as the thumb itself, with its back part a little narrower than its front part. The side of the leather that is smoothed in the tanning should be next to the string.

Thumb-tips are often made of the skin of horses or goats, or of other kinds of tanned hides, as well as of silver, copper, iron, bone and horn. The last variety is made by taking a fine horn, large enough to hold the thumb, and cutting it down to the right size; then a piece is carved out to expose the nail and the knuckle of the thumb, and a groove for the string is marked on the face of it. The same process is followed in making tips of silver or other metals.

The best thumb-tips, however, are made of leather of moderate thickness, neither too thick lest they interfere with the efficiency of shooting, nor too thin lest they fail to protect the thumb against the action of the string.

Leather tips are superior to those of silver and the other metals because they are soft and flexible and interfere least with the accuracy of shooting. Some archers, however, hold that tips of silver or of other metals are better than tips of leather in competitive and distance shooting. Ṭāhir al-Balkhi said that for distance shooting thick tips are better, while for accurate target shooting thin tips are superior. This is, in fact, correct.

XLIII. On shooting with the *ḥusbān*, *dawdan*, and *'uṣfūri* arrows through the hollow of a guide

THE Moslems, in their raids against the Turks, were wont to use the long arrow. But, whenever they missed, the Turks would pick up the arrow and shoot it back, inflicting serious injury upon the Moslems. In desperation, therefore, they held a council of war and vowed they would discover a method of shooting which would make it impossible for the Turks to return their arrows. After long study they evolved shooting with the *ḥusbān* arrow through the hollow of a guide. The Turks, having seen nothing like these small arrows, were unable to return them against the Moslems, who achieved several victories through the use of this new device. According to al-Ṭabari's statement, quoted by him on the authority of his Moslem masters, this was the reason for the invention and development of shooting with the *ḥusbān* (hailstone), *dawdan*, and *'uṣfūri* (birdlike) arrows through the hollow of a guide.

Others said that it was the Persians who invented the device. When the Persians, as a result of their fine and accurate marksmanship, defeated the Turks, the latter invented the shield for protection against the telling arrows of the Persians. This was suggested to the Turks when their king, having received a fish, noticed that its teeth were arranged one overlapping the other. He, therefore, got the idea of constructing shields consisting of different layers of gradually receding size laid one over the other. Armed with these new weapons they raided the Persians, whose arrows failed to penetrate the new protective device, and who were, consequently, defeated.

The Persians were then on the lookout for a stronger arrow to penetrate the Turkish shields and gradually developed the oblique method of shooting as well as the taking of their aim from the outside of the bow. This method resulted in the lengthening of the arrow and, therefore, in the increase of its driving force. Once the arrows became long and their force was increased as a result, the Persians were able to penetrate the Turkish shields. The Persians, accordingly, for the use of old men and youngsters who were unable to effect the long and hard draws resulting from the very long arrows, evolved shooting with the *ḥusbān* and *dawdan* arrows; thereby bringing up the driving force of their shots to a par with the shots of the strong men who could draw a long arrow to its full limit.

If this story is true—that the Persians developed the device for use against shields—then it might be said that shooting the *ḥusbān* and *dawdan* arrows through the hollow of a guide gives greater strength and driving force than shooting the long arrow. On the other hand, it might be said that they evolved this device and, after actual trial in combat, found it weak and ineffectual and were, consequently, driven to the development of the long arrow and the oblique stand in shooting, which, in fact, is the method current among them.

The *ḥusbān* and *dawdan* arrows are not used in stunts nor in any type of shooting except against shields and strong armor.

The Persians also developed shooting with stone balls, long iron needles with or without nocks, and with iron missiles known as "the beans of the prince" (*ḥimmaṣ al-amīr*), as well as hot needles and flaming arrows. All except the last are shot with the aid of a guide.

The guide (*majra*) is made of a trough that is one fist (which is the width of four fingers) longer than the archer's arrow; or the width of the hand when the fingers are arranged for the count of one (which is the width of three fingers) longer than the archer's arrow. It should be scooped out carefully, with a narrow opening and an interior slightly wider, so that the *ḥusbān* arrows can move freely in the hollow without being too loose. The size of the hollow should be as large as the end joint of the little finger, in order to permit free movement of the arrow, while the opening should be as wide as the arrow is at its nock end.[62]

The end of the guide which is toward the bowstring at the time of shooting should be slightly thinner than the other end and should also be pointed like a pen. Through this end a small hole is bored into which a strong string of silk or leather is inserted and made into a loop which fits around the little finger or the ring finger of the right hand at the time of shooting. Or, if the archer so desires, he can attach to the end of the string a small bead resembling the top of a spindle, and hold it between his little finger and ring finger at the time of shooting. Such a bead is better than the loop, because of the ease with which it can be released from between the fingers, especially in battle.

Guides are of four different kinds: square, round, hexagonal, and octagonal. The square kind is the best and simplest, especially for beginners and fighters. The round is good for target shooting and for practice, for which the hexagonal and octagonal are also suited.

62 Remember that the bulging Oriental nock is often the widest part of the arrow.

The best guides are those which are somewhat flattened at the place where they rest against the grip of the bow and, therefore, do not turn or move. The other side may still be round, or hexagonal, or octagonal. The guide which has a wide hollow and a narrow opening is superior and safer in the hands of a beginner, while one with a fairly wide opening offers a greater driving force.[63]

Guides are usually of hard, seasoned wood, free from moisture in order to avoid warping and contortion. They are also made of copper and iron, with narrow hollows, for the shooting of hot iron needles.

The manner of shooting with a guide consists in holding the bow by its grip with your left hand, while the string lies on the inside of your forearm which is toward your face [supinated; canting the bow anticlockwise]. You then place the guide on the grip of the bow at the *kabid* point, holding it in place with your left thumb. Next, take hold of the *ḥusbān* arrow with your right hand, insert it into the guide, and hold the guide and *ḥusbān* arrow firmly with your entire right hand. Then turn your left hand over and hold the bow as you would when shooting an ordinary long arrow. Place the guide in the bow and place the bead, if there be one, between your little finger and ring finger, or, if there be no bead, you insert either the little finger or the ring finger in the loop attached to the guide. Throughout this operation your right hand firmly holds the end of the guide and the *ḥusbān* arrow.

You then nock the *ḥusbān* arrow and hold it in place with the tip of either the index finger or middle finger of your left hand—lest the bowstring should push it—and lock your right hand upon the tip of the guide and the string together with sixty-three. Then take your left index finger off the *ḥusbān* arrow and your left thumb off the guide. Holding the grip of the bow in a good oblique grasp, draw as you would when shooting with a long ar-

[63] See Appendix, 14. The *majra* or Arrow Guide.

row, and aim as you would when shooting with a long arrow, either from the outside of the bow or from the inside.

Now draw the full length of the guide, exactly as you would have drawn if you had been shooting with a long arrow, and release as you would have released in that case; after which, you open your hand as when shooting in the normal way with a long arrow.

Swing the guide around above the central portion of your head with a good turn and bring the bowstring to rest [literally: put it to sleep] on the inside of your left forearm as you did at the beginning, place the guide on the grip of the bow, nock another *ḥusbān* arrow for another shot, and so on and on. The secret of this type of shooting lies in the speed and dexterity of the hands.

To shoot with the guide and repeat the operation successively there are five different ways, one of which we have already described as comprising the opening of the hand at the time of release and swinging the guide around the head.

The second consists of the following operation: After shooting with the guide you bring it back with your right hand off into your face and over against your left shoulder. You then raise it with your hand, place your hand upon your back, and swing it twice before your face as you would do with a sword in a tournament. Then bring the bowstring to rest on the inside of your forearm and place the guide against the grip as already described.

The third involves the following operation: When you shoot with the guide, hold it with your hand, hit its end lightly against the earth, then raise it with your right hand, swing it around, and place it against the grip as already described.

The fourth involves swinging it with speed immediately upon the conclusion of your shot, bringing it back, and pressing it down against the grip.

The fifth consists in employing both hands immediately upon the conclusion of the shot, bringing the guide and the grip together, the one upon the other.

The arrows shot with a guide are of three kinds: the first is known as the *ḥusbān*, the second as the *dawdan*, and the third as the *'uṣfūri*.

The *ḥusbān* is usually two spans and one phalanx in length, which is its maximum limit—the wood comprising two spans and the arrowhead the length of one phalanx. Some have said that it should be half the length of the ordinary arrow; others have insisted that it should be two spans in length including the arrowhead; while still others have maintained that it should be one and a half spans in length, which is its minimum limit. Those suitable for warfare should not exceed two spans in length including the arrowhead, and should not be shorter than one and a half spans. Those suitable for target shooting should be half the length of the ordinary arrow.

The *dawdan* should be one and one third spans in length including the arrowhead. Some said that it should be one span long excluding the arrowhead. Still others insisted that it should be one span long including the arrowhead; and others maintained that it should be two thirds of a span in length, which is its minimum limit.

The *'uṣfūri* should be two and a half phalanges in length, or two phalanges [the middle joint of the middle finger].

The kind of wood suitable for these arrows is heavy, hard, and strong. Likewise, the arrowheads should be heavy as light ones are worthless for these arrows.

Such arrows should weigh ten dirhams each; the wood and feathers weighing four dirhams, and the arrowhead six dirhams. According to others, the wood and feathers should weigh eight dirhams and the arrowhead four dirhams. Still others favor three dirhams for wood and feathers and five dirhams for the arrowhead. Ṭāhir, however, said that the wood and feathers should weigh two dirhams and the arrowhead six.

These weights govern the *ḥusbān* and the *dawdan*. The *'uṣfūri*, on the other hand, should weigh three dirhams, perhaps even less, and be of very thick wood. Its arrowhead should be designed to penetrate strong shields.

The best arrowheads for the guide arrows are the short round, the short triangular, and the long kinds of both. The best feathers are the soft and smooth. There should be two side feathers just outside the groove of the guide at the pen-shaped end, and a "male feather" (*dhakar*) in the hollow. This third feather should be long and low, never high lest it should get stuck within the guide and, consequently, militate against the driving force of the bow.

Iron needles, with nocks or without, hot or otherwise, can also be shot through the guide. Those with a nock are made in the shape of the *ḥusbān* arrows and vary, likewise, in size, according to the differences already mentioned in connection with the *ḥusbān*. The end of such a needle is either triangular or round and thick: slightly thicker than its own shaft. It is trimmed with three feathers with the aid of thread and tar. It is very good for penetrating shields and thrice reinforced armor and the like, which are otherwise difficult to penetrate.

Those which have no nocks have a greater driving force and a more telling penetration. The part where the nock should normally be is exactly like the rest of the stele. A special and separate nock is made for such an arrow from the tips of goat horns. Such nocks should not exceed the joint of a finger in length. Each is so turned that it is just as large as the opening of the guide. A hole is then bored transversely in its center. The size of the hole should be equal to the thickness of the string. A groove is then sawn obliquely from the end of the horn to the hole, which groove should also be as wide as the thickness of the string. This is nocked to the string at the time of shooting. Sometimes, however, the hole is bored through the horn piece, but no groove is sawn from the end of the horn to the hole. Instead, the horn piece is strung on the string before the bow is braced and before the eyes are made on the string. It remains there always. The first method is preferable since you can remove the horn piece from the string the moment you are through shooting.

The next steps are to make a hole in the end of the removable nock the size of the rear end of the needle you desire to shoot, insert the end of the needle into the hole, lock your fingers thereupon, draw, and shoot.

If you wish to shoot a hot needle, both the guide and the removable nock should be made of iron or copper. The needle is then heated and, with the aid of a pair of pliers, is laid in the guide and its end is inserted into the nock. Thence it is shot. Only such needles as have no nocks are heated and shot while hot. The part to be heated most is the arrowhead—the other part not being heated much lest the feathers be destroyed or the tar which holds the threads around the feathers be melted and thereby cause the feathers to become loose. In such cases it is better to hold the feathers in place with very fine copper wire.

XLIV. On stunt shooting

STUNT shooting is of two kinds; the first is carried out with the long arrow and the second with the short and other kinds of arrows that are shot through a guide.

The stunts that are done with one or more long arrows comprise fourteen different types.

The first of these is zone shooting (*ramy al-dārāt*), which is most telling against enemies. It consists of drawing a circle on the ground and then going away from it the distance of the cast of the bow, from which position you shoot upward, high into the air, toward the circle. When the arrow falls it should alight in the circle. You should practice this until you master it, say from a distance of one hundred cubits. You then come up twenty cubits nearer to the circle and again practice shooting up into the sky and having the arrow alight in the circle. Once you master the cast from that distance, you again come up twenty cubits closer and shoot again in the same way. You should continue your practice from successive points, each twenty cubits closer, until you can drop your arrow into the circle in that fashion from a distance of twenty cubits. If you can do that successfully, you shall have mastered the art of zone shooting: one of the most useful in storming towers and fortifications, where no other type of shooting would avail. In this way the arrows descend upon the enemy from above like crashing thunder while they are unaware. This will inflict great losses upon the enemy and will enable the Moslems to storm their strongholds successfully. Records show that a certain eastern city was stormed and occupied in this fashion.[64]

The second is shooting nockless arrows. The advantage

[64] To illustrate the value of this type of nearly vertical shooting, we will cite two well known historical examples:

In 1066, when William the Conqueror attacked the English near Hastings, the latter defended themselves by making a wall with their shields, which they interlocked and held with great power. Even cavalry could not break it. Then, as is clearly shown in the Bayeux Tapestry, the Norman archers shot high in the air so that the English were either obliged to raise their shields over their heads and thus break the wall or else be hit by the descending arrows, as was, in fact, the fate of King Harold.

The second incident occurred in 1096 during the Peasants' Crusade. The place was in Asia Minor about fifty miles southwest of Constantinople and the occasion was the rout which followed a disastrous defeat of the crusaders by the Turks. This quotation—slightly abbreviated—is from *The First Crusade*, by August C. Krey: "Above the shore of the sea was an ancient deserted fortress toward which three thousand pilgrims rushed in flight. They entered it in hope of defense, but, finding no gate, they piled up their shields and a huge mound of rocks in the doorway and bravely defended themselves with lances, wooden bows, and sling stones. But the Turks surrounded the fortress, which was without a roof, and aimed their arrows so high that they fell from the air in a shower and struck the enclosed Christians, killing the poor wretches."

in shooting nockless arrows lies in the fact that an enemy ignorant of the art cannot shoot them back at you. The operation consists in making your arrows in the ordinary way except for the nock, which should be left uncut, and, instead, the nock end of the arrow should be sharpened in the shape of the arrowhead. Place on the string some kind of ring which may be tied at the proper point with a strong thread. You then insert the rear end of the nockless arrow in the ring which will serve as a nock; draw, and shoot in the ordinary manner. In case of battle it is advisable to place on the string two or three such rings, one fixed at the proper point while the others remain loose to be used as spares in case the first one breaks.

Another method of shooting nockless arrows consists in placing on the string a small ring from which projects a nail-like extension known as *birūn*. The ring is strung onto the string loosely and can easily move upon it. When you employ ordinary arrows with normal nocks this device is not used; but when you intend to shoot nockless arrows you bore, instead of the nock, in the place where the nock should be, a hole big enough for the *birūn*. Then insert the *birūn* into the hole, lock your fingers, draw, and shoot.[65]

The third is the shooting of flaming arrows, which are

[65] That these two types of nockless arrows are practicable is proven by the fact that both of them were independently invented by Earl Mead of Cleveland, Ohio, and patented by him in 1930. The application for that patent lies before us and the following descriptions are taken from it.

1. The nock end of the arrow is tapered conically and fits into a metal seat, or ring, which is set in the string and tied there.

2. "A streamline arrow in which for the arrow-nock there is substituted an axial opening in the arrow which receives a projecting member integral with the bowstring seat." The bowstring seat may be either movable or immovable on the string. In a specimen that we saw, the seat was of brass and the pin was a piece of thin wire nail about a quarter of an inch in length. Excellent scores were made with arrows of this type but the odd nocks did not catch the popular fancy and their manufacture was soon discontinued.

The word *birūn* is Persian and means "a projection." As it was a foreign word to the author, it is retained here without translation to denote this previously nameless object.

called spindle-shaped, and are used for incendiary purposes, to set fire to the place where they fall. Such arrows are made by constructing a hollow arrowhead consisting of a number of tubes the ends of which are brought together. The interior of the arrowhead should be hollow, like the interior of the spindles women use. This is why it is called spindle-shaped. It should also have a cylindrical extension into which the shaft is inserted.

You mix some straw and cotton together and make them into a ball. Then you saturate the ball with tar and insert it into the hollow of the arrowhead. Then you bring it next to a flame, and shoot it as soon as it begins to burn. It will spring into a flaming projectile and will start a fire wherever it falls.

You may also take some otter fat, wax, black sulphur, bdellium gum [*Webster's International Dictionary*: "A gum resin obtained from *Commiphora africana*, similar to myrrh and used for the same purposes."], the pith of fresh cherry seeds—if you cannot obtain this, you may use cocoanut milk, and if this is not to be found, you may use the sap of wild figs—and a piece of quicklime untouched by water; you then grind the whole together, knead the mass with pure oil of balsam, roll it into small, pebble-like granules, and dry them. When you wish to shoot, sprinkle the granules with powdered black sulphur and shoot them with a stiff, strong bow, at night or by day, without bringing them next to a flame or fire. As each travels through the air it springs into flame. Al-Ṭabari has declared this to be true and that it has been practiced by experts in Egypt.

The fourth is sound-shooting, where you shoot at something you hear but do not see. When at night in the dark you hear something, brace your bow, nock your arrow, and prepare to shoot, having your left hand directly in front of your face and your left upper arm cleaving to your left cheek; then listen to the sound, and when you have determined the direction of its source, draw quickly and shoot.

It has been related that a certain king had a bodyguard consisting of twelve archers. On one of his trips by night they heard a suspicious sound and immediately shot their arrows. It turned out to be a dog, and all their twelve arrows were planted in its body.[66]

The fifth is shooting with the so-called *fard* or *qīrāṭ* into the earth, especially when the object at which you are shooting is in a well, cistern, or a deep and narrow place. To accomplish this, take a *fard* or *qīrāṭ*, place it in the earth opposite your left hand, stand upright with your feet close together, reach for a soft bow free from recurvature, string it, nock upon the string a thick and heavy arrow—since it is better hitting—and draw toward your face. When you have drawn half the length of the arrow, you turn over your left hand very quickly and, at the same time, swing your right hand up over your head until your right forearm lies on your back in line with the side of your neck; after which, you push your left hand downward along your left thigh—thereby completing the draw to the full length of the arrow—and simultaneously lean with your neck toward the *fard* or *qīrāṭ*. On completing the full draw, release and let the arrow go.

Another very unusual and dangerous way, and, therefore, one to be attempted only by experts who are adept at it, consists in using the tip of the foot for a *fard* or *qīrāṭ* and removing it the instant the arrow is released. If you should remove your foot first, your aim would be spoiled; on the other hand, if you were a moment late in removing your foot, you would hit it with the arrow. The secret of its success, therefore, lies in removing the foot and releasing the arrow at exactly the same instant.[67]

66 The face of a person with normal hearing automatically turns toward a sound in order to balance the tonal quality in both ears. By thus holding the bow arm extended directly before the face, and with the head immobilized on the neck by the pressure of the upper arm on the left cheek, the arrow is likely to be well directed when the range is short.

67 See Appendix, 15. Meaning of *fard* and *qīrāṭ*.

The sixth is what is known as hoof-shooting and is staged by leading a horse into a place completely free of any hoof marks. You then take a soft bow free of recurvature and, stringing it, take five fine arrows the feathers of which are a little far from their nocks. Place them in your right hand; holding them next to their nocks with your little finger, ring finger, and middle finger, similar to the count of nine, or, if you so desire, you may hold them between these three fingers. With your thumb and index finger you then push one of these arrows so that its nock lies in the palm of your hand, and nock it. Then, holding the grip of the bow with your left hand, place it at the base of the tail of your horse, on the right if you are right-handed, that is, if you draw with your right hand, or at the base of the tail on the left if you are left-handed. Shoot at the marks of the hoof on the earth, repeating the operation quickly as the horse is on the run. The stunt is useful in the event that you are followed by a lion or any other beast of prey which might hang to your mount. A shot would disentangle the beast.

The seventh is shooting birds while they are flying. Birds are either fast flying or slow flying. To shoot the fast flying birds, like pigeons and martins, other than accidentally is practically impossible. It is a fruitless effort, based on no principle. But the shooting of slow flying birds with wings outstretched, like storks, eagles, vultures, and the like, is a possible pursuit based on definite principles which may be mastered after painstaking practice as prescribed by experts. This is performed as follows: Take two long posts, as tall as you can find and stick them in the earth about twenty cubits apart. String a line between them and fasten to it a flat object about the size of a bird. Then mount your horse with your bow ready in your hand, and as you approach a point exactly below the line, lean your head over your shoulder, take aim, draw, and shoot. All this should be done while the horse is on the run. When you have mastered this stunt you should be able to shoot the flying bird, since this method provides shooting while the archer is on the move and the target is still and stationary, whereas in shooting the flying bird, the reverse is the case: the archer is still and stationary while the target is on the move. If you possess no mount, practice the same operation while running on foot; and if you happen to be averse to running because of the effort, practice by shooting directly at the flying bird until you have mastered the stunt. If the bird be a stork, an eagle, or a vulture—birds the wings of which are usually outstretched—aim at the tip of its beak, draw quickly, and release without any pause. If it be one of the birds the wings of which are not usually outstretched, or a bird which is neither slow nor fast in its flight, like a crane or a crow, aim at a point about one cubit in front of its beak, draw quickly and release without any pause. Even then there is no guarantee of uniform accuracy, because the winds often interfere with the flight of the arrow.

The eighth is shooting the edge of the sword. It consists in taking a sword and planting its hilt firmly in the earth while its edge remains above the earth. You then make for yourself full-bodied arrows with tips thicker than their steles and leave them without arrowheads. Their ends, where normally the arrowheads are fixed, should be cut straight and even without being pointed. You next take a soft bow free of recurvature, fitted with a fairly thick string, and stand facing the edge of the sword squarely. If your shot be accurate, the arrow will be split in twain by the edge of the planted sword. You may also try the same thing while on the back of a galloping horse, shooting several arrows in succession against the edge of the sword.

The ninth is ring shooting, consisting in planting a cane into the earth at an inclined angle, and, with the aid of a hair, hanging a ring or signet from the top of the cane. Another hair to which is tied a small piece of lead should be dangled from the ring or signet in order to weigh it down and thereby avoid having it tossed by the wind. Then with a soft bow fitted with a thick string and a heavy arrow you shoot from a distance of twenty-five cubits—the shortest permissible range in target shooting.

The tenth is hair shooting, and consists in planting a cane into the earth at an inclined angle, and hanging from its top a hair weighed down with a small piece of lead. Shoot against it with a soft bow fitted with a thick string and a heavy arrow. The arrowhead should, however, be wide and very sharp. If, because of the distance, you are unable to see the hair, you can aim at the dangling piece of lead.

The eleventh is lamp shooting, and consists in lighting a candle or a lamp, placing it at a reasonable distance, and shooting at its flame with a heavy, square-headed, and copious arrow—heavily feathered—and a soft bow with a thick string; thereby putting the flame out without upsetting the candle or the lamp, whichever it may be.

The twelfth is shooting the returning arrow: an arrow which, as it travels on its flight, suddenly returns to the point whence it was shot, and may even hit the archer himself. Such an arrow is made by shaving a shaft evenly and forcing it through a ring so that it emerges perfectly uniform. You then cut into it two nocks, one on each end, and thin each end down a little. Trim it with eight feathers, four at each end next to a nock, placing each feather on the one end opposite to a feather on the other, in the same alignment. You next bore in the center of the groove of each nock a small hole, filling the one with lead and leaving the other empty. Nock the arrow on the end which has been filled with lead and shoot it with the bow-hand raised as high as your head. No sooner does it reach the limit of its flight than it swerves and returns to the point whence it was shot. If it should fail to return to the place where you were standing when you shot it, know that you were not exact in its construction.

In describing the returning arrow, al-Ṭabari stated that its middle part should be thinned down but failed to mention anything concerning the hole in each nock or the lead filling of the one and the emptiness of the other. If his description should work, then the thinning of the middle part of the arrow would take the place of the two holes and the lead in one of them. Otherwise, it would be better to follow the first description and to ignore the additional remarks of al-Ṭabari. The purpose of such an arrow is to deceive an enemy who happens to be at your side, and to shoot him while he is unaware.[68]

The thirteenth is shooting a sidewise arrow. This is one that leaves the bow with the usual straight flight (that is, with the arrowhead pointing forward and the nock to the rear) but which soon rotates laterally on its center of gravity, so that it proceeds in its course broadside on (that is, with the head to one side, the nock to the other, and the middle of the shaft following the original line of aim).

The sidewise arrow is made by carefully shaving the shaft so that both ends are tapered like a pencil, gradually increasing in size from the ends to the middle, where it should be thickest. Its nock should also be very thick, and it should be trimmed with three feathers, one of which should be higher than the other two. If, on shooting this arrow it should fail to go sidewise, the failure will be because the nock is too light, and it should, therefore, be made heavier. This can be done by boring a small hole in the middle of the groove of the nock and filling it with lead.

Al-Ṭabari concurred in the description of the sidewise arrow, namely, that it should be thick in the middle and taper off gradually and evenly toward both ends, where it should be thin; but he also added that it should have nei-

68 See Appendix, 16. The Returning Arrow.

ther feathering nor an arrowhead, and failed to mention anything concerning making its nock heavier. He said, however, that if you wish to shoot such an arrow and have it go sidewise as described, you should nock it not in the usual place on the string, in line with the *kabid*, but on a point about a span above the *kabid*.

What we have related on the authority of others than al-Ṭabari is probably more accurate, since an arrow cannot travel straight without feathers.[69] How then could it travel sidewise without them?

This method of shooting is useful for hunting flocks of small birds. Birds which have been killed in this manner are unlawful to eat, since they have, in effect, been beaten to death. Those which have been hit by the arrowhead, however, and the mention of the name of God having preceded the shot, are lawful to eat.

The fourteenth is the trap arrow. It is made by shaving an arrow evenly except at the place of the feathers, where it should be thinned down and fletched with three or four vanes. At about one span from the front end of the shaft, two holes should be bored crosswise, one above the other and very close. The two, however, should never meet lest the shaft be thereby weakened and consequently be broken when used. You then take two small branches that measure about half a span each and force them into the two holes so as to form, as it were, a cross. You then join their ends with a ring made of bamboo, or pomegranate, or quince wood, or the like (wood which is flexible), inserting the ends of the two small branches into the wood of the ring or, if you so desire, tying them with thread or twine. Such an arrow is useful for hunting small birds. Here again only those birds that are hit by the arrowhead are lawful to eat.

The second kind of stunt shooting treats of using the short arrow with a guide. It comprises two types.

The first type consists of taking a strong and hard stave

[69] See Appendix, 17. Featherless Arrows.

and making of it a fairly thick arrow: slightly thicker than the normal variety and one fist longer, nockless and featherless. Its end where the arrowhead would normally be should be thick and round, in the shape of a walnut, turned and hollowed like a funnel. The hollow should be about one finger joint in depth and in width the size of the shot that will be used therein. This funnel-like head should then be bound about with a ring of either copper or iron. Near the rear end, about a finger joint removed from it, a hole the size of the string should be bored through the shaft, and a slot wide enough to take the string should be sawn obliquely from one side to the hole. It is sawn obliquely to prevent the string from falling out at the time of shooting. When this is done, make for the funnel-like head of the arrow iron shots of appropriate size, large enough to fill its cavity; fix the arrow on the string through the oblique slot leading to the hole; grasp the bow by the grip; place the shot in the cavity of the head; draw to the extent of your normal drawing with a long arrow; and finally release. The string will snap back while still remaining in the hole of the arrow and the shot will be catapulted from its cavity with force and speed. The arrow, however, will remain attached to the string. You may, if you so desire, make a nock for the arrow and attach it to the string with a strong silk thread or the like, instead of the hole and slot. On shooting therewith, the thread prevents the arrow itself from being shot along with the iron missile.[70]

[70] This apparatus will certainly work, although we have found that so much force is absorbed by the shaft which is attached to the string that the missile does not fly nearly so far as when it is shot from the *majra* which is described on the pages immediately following. However, the archer soon finds that there is an unmentioned factor which places his bow in the greatest jeopardy. All bows are built to withstand a strain in one direction only, that is, the bend toward the archer, and when the bow is loosed in normal shooting and the arrow leaves it at its position of rest, the bow receives no further strain beyond a jarring that is well within its limits of safety. But the attached shaft introduces an enormous stress in the wrong direction, which the bow is not built to withstand. Instead of

This type of arrow could also be used for shooting the missile known as the beans of the prince (*ḥimmaṣ al-amīr*). This projectile consists of a triangular piece of iron the size of a finger joint, with three spikes on each of its three sides. When it falls to the ground, the spikes on one of its three sides are planted into the earth while the spikes of the other two sides stick up and serve as barbed obstacles: inflicting injury on man or beast. This missile is shot exactly as are the other iron shots and is usually aimed at narrow and crowded places.

The same type of arrow could be used for shooting eggs, a useless thing in itself. In order to avoid breaking the egg, the cavity of the head of the arrow should be cushioned with a pad of cotton. If, on the other hand, an egg were carefully emptied through a small hole made in one end and then filled with tar, it could be shot against any object which you might wish to burn down. That object would thus be smeared with tar, and the next step would consist of shooting against the tar-smeared object a flaming arrow, which would set it ablaze.

By making the funnel-shaped head of the arrow of copper or iron, with a tubular extension wherein the shaft is inserted, you can shoot red-hot iron balls and thereby set on fire any place that is otherwise inaccessible.

The second of the two types of shooting with a guide is superior to the first and better for the bow. It is done by taking a thick stick, turning it evenly, and thinning down the end which rests against the string to an extent which will enable you to lock your fingers thereon. You then polish it and carve on one of its sides a groove extending

the string's being freed after the loose it is given a terrific yank toward the bow, which pulls the tips toward the grip and, in combination with more complicated stresses, may even break one limb off near the handle. We had this happen to an excellent osage bow. Whether or not other types of fracture might occur we have not had enough experience to say. The voluntary statement of the author that the second type of shooting with a guide was "better for the bow" suggests that he, too, had witnessed similar mishaps.

from one end to the other, similar to the groove of the guide from which the *ḥusbān* arrows are shot and in size the thickness of the string or two thirds thereof.[71] To each end you fix a ring of iron or copper, while on the thinned end you attach a strong silk thread with either a loop which goes around your little finger or ring finger, or with a little wooden bar which catches between these two fingers, similar to what you use in the case of the *ḥusbān* arrows. The shaft would then have along one of its sides a groove extending from one ring to the other. Now, take the tip of a horn and make of it a nock half a finger joint in length, and just thick enough to move freely in the groove from one end to the other. Then drill a hole transversely through it as thick as the string and cut from the side of the nock to the hole an oblique slot by means of a saw. Then set the string against the guide and fix the nock on the string. Insert the shot or missile, which has been made with a head as wide as the groove of the shaft, into that groove; lock your fingers on the guide; draw the limit; and release. The string will carry the nock and the nock will hit the shot, which will emerge like a shooting star. This type is among the wonders of the profession.[72]

Should you desire to shoot hot missiles, you should make your guide of iron or copper. The guide could also be made of cane in which you make a groove from one end to

[71] All the Oriental bowstrings that we have seen have been two or three times as thick as ordinary American strings.

[72] The rings of iron or copper that are fastened at each end of the *majra* are for the purpose of preventing the shuttlelike "nock," or horn-piece, from leaving the groove. The rear one is not indispensable but the forward one is of great importance. We found it better practice to set this ring back a few inches from the extreme end, where it could be reached by the shuttle without undue strain to the bow while the tip of the *majra* was still resting on the bow-hand and bow.

The word "hit" is rather indecisive. The missile certainly can be pushed all the way along the groove from the limit of the draw but, on the other hand, it is possible to tuck the missile under the front ring and let it receive a hammerlike blow from the shuttle nock. In fact, this principle of the blow was finally adopted in crossbows as providing a greater propulsive force than the long push.

the other, and around each end whip strong twine or sinew with glue to produce a ringlike effect. You should first remove the exterior bark of the cane in order to be able to whip the twine tightly and to make it possible for the glue to stick firmly.

Through this device the so-called bird arrows are shot. This is done by taking a stave a little thicker than that which has already been described, and making of it a guide which is similar to the one already described but with a larger cavity. You should then attach to it a cord—with or without a wooden bar—and cut for it a hollowed socket the size of the cavity of the guide so that it can move freely from one end to the other. A loop should be attached to the socket and fastened to the bowstring so that the socket will not leave the guide at the time of shooting. Fill the socket with the bird arrows (*'uṣfūri*) which, as we have already stated, are two or two and a half finger joints in length. Insert the socket in the cavity of the guide; lock your fingers on the end of the guide, and at the same time hold the cord and bar in your locked fingers; draw, and then release. The string snaps against the socket and the arrows are thus driven out in a group similar to flying birds. The arrows thus shot may be five, six, or even ten in number. They should be placed in the socket evenly with their arrowheads straight; otherwise their flight will be no good.

Oftentimes the socket is made solid, not hollowed; instead, ten holes are made in it for the arrows. These holes penetrate nearly but not quite through the socket, and should be wide enough to enable the arrows to be inserted freely therein but not so wide as to cause them to slant one way or the other. They are best shot against a shield, thereby resulting in a banging sound.

You can also shoot them out like Numidian birds, led by one called the leader or guide. This is done by inserting in the socket a larger arrow, longer than the rest. When shot with the others it precedes them, while they follow in its wake. Or you may have all the arrows the same size and half stop the middle hole with wood, making it half as deep as the others. When shot, the middle arrow leads the others by half a length.[78]

Or, by making the opening of the socket narrower than the rest of its cavity, you may shoot therewith sand or water, which shoots out in a column and then sprays in every direction. Such a stunt is useful for blinding the eyes of enemies in narrow places and at night. It is often performed as a stunt before kings and princes.

XLV. Targets and target practice

THE first thing a novice should do is to practice shooting against targets of all kinds: near and far, still and moving.

STILL TARGETS

The first type is that of the "imitation horseman" and is done as follows: Take a staff the height of a mounted horseman; attach to its upper end a disk about a span in diameter, representing the horseman's head; one span below the disk place a shield about three spans in diameter, representing the shield of the horseman. The target is then

[78] As with so many of these stunts, we had to try this one out in order to see just what the author meant. Our attempts were successful but the thing is nothing more nor less than a toy. We cannot conceive of its serving any useful purpose as the cast of the outflying bird arrows is not great and accurate aim is impossible. The socket must have a cavity of about one and a half inches to hold ten small arrows, and, if its wall is one eighth of an inch in thickness, the groove of the *majra* should be fully two inches square to allow free movement and let the arrows out under the terminal ring.

We also made a shuttle nock which was surmounted by a crosspiece that rode on top of the *majra* and contained holes about one inch in depth to contain the nock ends of the arrows. It worked all right, but the *majra* must then be shot on the right side of the bow in the Oriental fashion to keep the crosspiece from hitting the hand. We believe that the first type is the one the author had in mind.

placed at a distance equivalent to the cast of the bow. Thus placed, the novice should shoot against the shield with five arrows. When he can shoot the entire five arrows in succession without missing a single shot, he should then proceed to shoot against the "head" in a similar fashion. He should continue with this practice until he perfects his aim.

The second type of still target is that of the "opposing targets." It consists in placing four targets: one to your right, another to your left, a third in front of you, and a fourth behind you. You then stand in the center, holding four arrows between the fingers of your right hand. Starting with the one on your right and moving on to the one behind you, then the one on your left, and finally the one in front of you, you shoot at each while standing with your feet planted firmly on the ground and not moving from their place at all. The only part of your body which moves throughout the operation is your waist, which pivots around to whatever direction you may be shooting.

When after days, even months, of practice, this operation is perfected, start to practice the same thing while mounted on a calm and steady horse. When this is perfected, start to practice the same while your horse is moving between the targets. Finally, when you become adept at this, hitting the target every time you shoot, start practicing the same thing while your horse is running at full speed. When this stunt is perfected, you have attained the limit toward which every archer sets his eyes. This is, however, not possible except through perseverance and continued practice.

MOVING TARGETS

The first type of moving target is what is known as "imitation beast on a chariot." It consists of constructing a four-wheeled chariot, and tying firmly on its fore part a skin stuffed with straw and behind it a small skin stuffed likewise. The front and larger skin represents the beast to be shot. The hind and smaller skin represents the archer's dog which usually chases the beast. You then pull the chariot up a hill, and on reaching the top push it down the steep incline. As the chariot rolls down the hill you start to shoot at the front skin. If you hit, then you have hit the beast it represents; but if your arrow hit the hind skin which represents the dog you have hit your own dog, thereby killing it and missing the beast you wished to shoot.

Instead of the stuffed skins, some have recommended the drawing of pictures on the chariot to represent a lion and a dog. This is, however, an oversight since it is unlawful to draw any pictures of life. The Apostle said: "Those who draw pictures shall be tormented at the day of resurrection, and shall be told: 'Bring to life what ye have fashioned.' " The Apostle also said: "Verily the angels shall enter a house containing statues." The learned have agreed that every likeness which casts a shadow and is in the form of something endued with life is unlawful to fashion or to draw. They did, indeed, differ on drawings which cast no shadow, like those on walls and tapestries and rugs. This is, however, outside the scope of the present discussion.

Another type is that of ball shooting. For this purpose make a ball of wood, neither large nor small, and wrap it in rags. It is then tied with a fairly long rope to the back of the saddle. The horseman archer spurs his mount to full speed and, turning in his saddle, shoots at the rolling and jumping ball. He should continue to practice this stunt until it is mastered.

SHOOTING A HORSEMAN

If the horseman be galloping toward you, aim at his saddle bow. Should the arrow swerve high it will hit the horseman's chest; should it fall low it will alight in his belly. If, on the other hand, the horseman be running away from you, aim at the back of his saddle. Should the arrow swerve high it will hit the horseman's back; and should it fall low it will alight on the back of his mount.

If one of the two be standing still and the other rushing against him to run him down, the former should aim his arrow at the neck of the horse. It will alight either in the rider's chest or between the eyes of the horse. In the event of the horseman's running away, the archer who is standing stationary should aim at the horseman's head. Should the arrow swerve high it will alight between the horseman's shoulders; should it fall short it will hit either the base of his back or the mount itself. All this requires practice and perseverance.

ON SHOOTING LIONS

One should not attempt to shoot a lion except from the back of a trained and reliable mount, agile in its forward and backward movements. Its tail should either be well combed or, what is still better, shaved—in order to avoid the possibility of having the lion plant his claws therein. If the lion should attack you, toss at him some shawl or garment. He will be busied therewith and you will be able to move away from him a distance of about one hundred cubits, dependent upon the speed of your mount. Then turn around and shoot. If he should rush toward you again, run before him zigzag fashion. This makes it difficult for the lion to overtake you. If he starts to fall back, turn around from a distance of about seventy cubits and shoot. If he tries to assault you for a third time, continue to run away from him, zigzag fashion, until he is tired and worn out. You then approach him as near as possible, dependent upon the degree of his fatigue, and shoot. Even then you should be on the alert, never trusting him until you have actually riddled him with your arrows.

Some maintain that a lion will never rush against a hunter so long as his tail remains hoisted upwards. Only when he lowers his tail does he attack.

Others suggest that a manacle made of hair and saturated with tar should be tossed at the lion when he is furious and therefore suspicious. He is apt to take it up with his claws, which will then become entangled therein. Thereupon, shoot, and with God's good luck you will succeed.

ON SHOOTING "TENS" OF LONG ARROWS

Take light, hard, and strong wood, and make therefrom arrows perfectly fashioned, thin throughout, with fine nocks and very fine arrowheads. Some have even suggested that the arrowheads be made of the quills of eagle feathers affixed to the thicker ends of the shafts. Each complete arrow should weigh three dirhams.

When ten such arrows are ready, you place them in order upon the string, one on top of the other. Stretch open the fingers of your right hand and insert the string between the middle and the ring fingers, while all the digits except the thumb are inside the bow and the thumb is outside it. At the grip the arrows are placed along it, resting upon the index finger of the left hand. Then hold the grip firmly and straight, while the left thumb is stretched erect and pressed against the arranged arrows to hold them in place, one on top of the other. You then lock upon it by inserting the string between the index finger and thumb of the drawing hand right at the base, holding the index finger down beside the nocks of the different arrows inside the bow and the thumb in a similar fashion from the outside of the bow. The lock should be twenty, edgewise. Draw and release. The arrows will emerge like a single arrow and alight upon the target thereby making it look like a porcupine. No one should attempt this stunt unless he is an expert therein.

An archer wishing to learn this stunt should start with two arrows and gradually increase the number until he attains to ten. The secret of its mastery consists in the careful fashioning of the arrows, their thinness, their lightness, their arrangement at nocking, and in holding them in place with the thumb of the left hand so that they may not move nor have their arrangement disturbed.

Archers have disagreed concerning the type of draw that should be used, as it may depend upon the length or shortness of the fingers. It is best for each individual to determine the draw best suited to his fingers and use it.[74]

ON SHOWER, OR SUCCESSIVE, SHOOTING

For this stunt one should use fine arrows that are pared thin at their nocks and are fletched with four vanes set a little way off from the nock at a distance of about two finger joints. In every arrow you may have two nocks intersecting each other crosswise at right angles. This makes it easier to nock an arrow with great speed and without looking at the nock or string. [See page 18.]

To shoot such an arrow, place it first in the palm of your

[74] Complicated, difficult, and confusing as this description seems to be, it can be resolved to reasonable simplicity when put to the actual test of shooting. To explain the text, we would begin by saying that the bow-hand had better be held palm up with the bow horizontal while the arrows are being laid upon it and nocked, as in this prone position they lie side by side and so do not become jumbled. However, they will also remain in place if the bow is inclined backward somewhat, but less than the horizontal. The string is then taken deep between the middle and ring fingers, not with the intention of drawing, but simply that the arrows may be steadied by the fingers until they can be supported against the side of the bow by the elevation and pressure of the left thumb. In our experiments we could cover only seven arrows with the left thumb, but with thinner shafts, a longer thumb, and more practice, it is probable that another archer could increase the number to the required ten. When the left thumb has obtained a good lateral pressure on the arrows, the bow is held erect. Then the temporary grip on the string—which kept the nocks from slipping off—is removed and for a moment the right hand is not engaged at all. Then the lock, or draw, or clench, of twenty—in which the thumb is laid between the first two fingers—is placed on the string. If it is done "edgewise"—which would seem to mean the edge of the hand on top—all the fingers can play a part in holding the nock ends steadily against the string. As the author allows, some archers may do better with other locks.

hand and then hold its nock[75] beneath your fingers—the little finger, the ring finger, and the middle finger—in a way resembling the count of nine. The arrowhead should point to the ground. You then slam its middle point, or the point marking a third of its length from the head, against the grip of the bow and, at the same time, push the arrow with the palm of your hand and receive it with your index finger and thumb. Then nock it, draw, and release. Others have said that it is better to slam the arrowhead against the grip.

This should be practiced until it is mastered completely. Then you add another arrow, placing both in the palm of your hand and holding their two nocks beneath your fingers—the little finger, the ring finger, and the middle finger—in a way resembling the count of nine. You then slam the arrowhead of one of them, or its middle point, or the point marking a third of its length, against the grip, and at the same time push the arrow with the palm of your hand and receive it with your index finger and thumb. Then nock, draw, and release.

While this operation is being done, the other arrow will still be held with the little finger. After the first is released you push this second arrow with the palm of your hand and receive it with the index finger and thumb. Then nock, draw, and release. This should also be practiced until it is perfected. Then you may add a third arrow and do the same. When this is mastered, a fourth and a fifth arrow may be added; and so on.[76]

[75] It is rather unfortunate that, in English, the word *nock* is used to mean two different things: the notch and the end of the arrow which contains the notch.

[76] We have tried this method of quick repetition in shooting and are convinced that it can be mastered by practice, though it is very difficult for one who is not trained to the thumb draw and shooting from the right side of the bow. It could not be applied to the European manner of shooting from the left side. The fundamental idea is that the drawing hand holds several arrows tucked away toward the outer edge of the palm and held there by the three fingers mentioned. Then, by successive movements of the

Another way to do this stunt is by placing the arrows between the fingers of the right hand thus: the nock of each arrow between two fingers when the arrows are only three; if they be six, then place two arrows between each two fingers; or if they be nine, three arrows between each two fingers; or more as you are able. Then follow the rest of the operation as described in the previous paragraphs.

A third way, which is faster than the two already mentioned, consists of taking three or six arrows, depending on your ability, and placing their middle points between the fingers of your drawing hand, while their nocks and feathers are along the inner side of your forearm. You then proceed in the manner described under the first method of shooting shower arrows.

The first method, however, is the best because it is possible to effect a clench therein, unlike the others which preclude the clench because of the position of the arrows between the fingers. It has already been stated that the clench is among the main principles of good shooting.

A fourth method of shooting shower arrows has been described by some professionals. This consists of placing the bundle of arrows in the left hand and gripping it along with the handle of the bow. But this is indeed wrong and results in no shower shooting. It is wrong because it renders the grip weak. It results in no shower shooting because the archer will have to release his hand in order to bring the next arrow into a shooting position.

It is best for the beginner to practice these movements first without attempting to shoot. When he has mastered them, he may proceed to the actual shooting.

According to al-Ṭabari, some have maintained that the

palm which are almost instinctive, one arrow after another is allowed to be taken hold of by the index finger and thumb, nocked, drawn, and released, while the other arrows still are held in the palm of the drawing hand awaiting their turn. The word "slam" may be a translation of excessive meaning, but it is intended to convey the idea of a very rapid movement and is difficult to supplant with a better one.

first man to evolve this method of shooting, namely, the shower or successive shooting, was Busṭām. He is supposed to have seen one day a hawk attacking a stork, swooping down upon it and flying away, and swooping down again, and so on until the stork was killed. This is supposed to have given him the idea of repeated attacks from which he evolved the shower or successive shooting.

Others said that Kisra once ordered Busṭām to shoot a lion in his presence. One arrow, however, failed to kill the beast, and Kisra exclaimed that an arrow was not a satisfactory weapon; unlike a sword with which one can strike one blow after another, or a spear with which one can thrust repeatedly. Once the arrow is released it is gone and the archer needs another. The interval between each two shots might endanger the safety of the warrior or the hunter. Busṭām gave thought to the matter and subsequently devised the shower or successive shooting, with five, ten, or fifteen arrows, all held at the same time in the archer's hand. They are shot one after the other in rapid succession thereby rendering the bow and arrow superior to the sword and spear, because no one could possibly strike ten simultaneous blows with the sword or ten simultaneous thrusts with the spear as you would do with the shower arrows.

Al-Ṭabari said that he himself had shot in this fashion fifteen arrows, one after the other in rapid succession. This is the best type of shooting and there is nothing beyond it in power or accuracy, and no one can manage to do it except a person who has trained himself in it and has obtained mastery in it and also in horsemanship. The kings of Persia were wont to take children and teach it to them, rewarding those who mastered it and punishing those who did not.

Archery is the best weapon of horsemen, and the best among them have not ceased to confess their inability to oppose an archer.

XLVI. Quivers, belt, arrow picker, file

A QUIVER should be made of leather, felt, or wood; but the best is that made of leather. It should have a wide opening and should gradually become narrower down to near the bottom, where it should become wide again like the top. It should have a cover to shield the feathers from possible rain. In size, it should hold from twenty-five to thirty arrows, which is the limit of capacity. Some archers have held that its length should be three spans but this is wrong because the usual length of arrows is nine handbreadths (which are three spans) or ten handbreadths (which are three and one third spans). If the quiver were three spans deep, the feathers would be within it and would be spoiled because of it, especially if the arrows were made after the school of those who place the feathers as far as two digits from their nocks. The correct thing, therefore, is what we have described; namely, that it should reach to the lower limit of the feathers. Every archer should have his quiver of this length, that is, up to the feathers of his own arrows. The quiver therefore varies with the length or shortness of its arrows. It sometimes reaches three spans or more according to the Persian school who shoot obliquely because their arrows are long, reaching twelve handbreadths in length (which is four spans). They place their feathers touching the nocks. The quiver should also be lined inside and outside.

The manner of carrying the quiver consists in having its strap over the left shoulder and the quiver itself hung along the right side of the back with its opening on a level with the right shoulder. It will not interfere with you in all your movements and all your pauses and all your shooting. Never place it in front of you along your shoulder, for it will interfere with your draw and with your sitting down and walking and running and all your movements and all your pauses and all your shooting.

The bow itself is on the left side in a case made of wood. The length of the bowcase should be the length of the bow or less by half a span, and it is measured by the bow when it is strung. Sometimes the archer may place his sword therein, along with his bow.

If you use a belt it should have two hooks: one on your right-hand side and one on your left-hand side. The belt is worn over your clothes. You hang the quiver from the hook which is on the right-hand side, with its top in front of you. The bowcase is hung from the left-hand hook. You secure them both firmly so that the top of the quiver will not tilt while you are running and let the arrows drop out, or the top of the bowcase also tilt and let the bow drop, especially when the case is shorter than the bow. Know ye also that the quiver of the expert holds twenty-five arrows. One should not, however, limit himself to that number in battle, but should carry others stuck in his boots up to the feathers and others stuck in his belt with their nocks level with his neck.

Every archer should also have an arrow picker, which consists of a stick a little thicker than the arrow and of about the same length. Into one end of the stick a slot is sawn to the depth of about a span. At the point marking the end of the slot a ring made of copper or sinew should be fixed with glue so that the stick will not split when it is used. Then the extremities of the slot are spread apart the thickness of the arrow, with the result that the slot, when placed on the ground, forms a triangle. An arrow can then be picked up by pressing this picker against it.

The archer should also have a pair of scissors for trimming the feathers and a file to enlarge the nock or sharpen the arrowhead whenever the need arises.

[Note: There now follow twenty-six pages which treat of betting, as governed by Moslem law. Most of the matter has nothing whatever to do with archery and the small part which has some relation, however remote, is concerned merely with legal questions as to how wagers should be laid.]

It is related that the Apostle was wont to be pleased with the man who had mastered swimming, archery and horsemanship. 'Umar [the second caliph] commanded that children be taught those three accomplishments. Said he: "Learn ye the Koran and archery; verily the best hours of the believer are those in which he remembers God."

Muḥammad ibn-al-Mawwāz said: "There is no harm in employing a man to teach you archery, horsemanship, combat, sword warfare, jumping to the back of a horse, wielding a spear, protecting with shields, throwing the javelin, and shooting with catapults, as well as anything else which may be of use against the enemy."

XLVII. Inscriptions on bows, arrows, and quivers

ON BOWS

SAID the poet:

> More dreaded by the dauntless foe
> Than any other warlike blow,
> Come the wooden shafts which are
> Shot with bows that send them far.
> They fell his ranks, line after line,
> And shower them with death divine.
> Piercing through the shield and mail,
> They cause the breath of life to fail.

And another:

> It falls to me to wield the bow and bend its limbs,
> Though in the act of death my arrow far excels it;
> For if to slay the foeman marks a weapon's rank,
> What can surpass that one which pierces through
> him?

And another:

Elegant in form and wonderful in structure!
When such a thing is sought, the Arab bow is found.
If enemies approach, it welcomes them with arrows,
Laden with death and bearing fear and awe.
Such is the Arab bow, with victory bound of God;
His holy writ and revelation with its arrows spreading.

ON ARROWS

Said the poet:

An arrow from a warrior,
Shot at an unbeliever,
Counts more than many prayers
Said by a pious hermit.

ON QUIVERS

Said the poet:

I am full of fatal arrows;
My merchandise is death and pain.
Learn by what thou hast seen of me.
I am the blight of the wide world.

APPENDIX

1. REINFORCED BOWS

At first glance this bow might seem to be identical with the composite bow which is described on page 13 but we believe that there is a fundamental difference. In all probability, the *mu'aqqabah* was essentially a wooden bow, of the general type and nature of wooden bows, which was strengthened by the addition of horn and sinew. That is to say, specifically, that inasmuch as the wood was the chief component it would be too thick to be bent acutely without fracture unless it were well over five feet in length—even nearer to six feet—and the bow would be nearly, or quite, straight when it was unbraced. Such bows have existed elsewhere at various times and, while they often show some reflexion, or bending toward the back when unbraced, the curve is gradual, regular, and conservative—more like the arc of a large circle; it is never the sharp, angular, and exaggerated reflexion which is one of the dominant characteristics of the true composite bow.

Why the reinforced bow was "used only by experts and those who live near water," is obscure. The first phrase may imply that their greater strength would require the well developed musculature of an expert to control them adequately. The second may refer to atmospheric humidity. Although too much dampness may soften the sinew and thus reduce the power of either a reinforced or a composite bow, too much dryness can make them weak and also brittle, chiefly by destroying the colloidal nature of the glue. In our personal collection of composite bows from Korea, China, and India are several which have been utterly ruined by the dryness of the air in our steam-heated American houses. Some have almost completely lost their cast and some have broken when they were drawn because of separation and buckling of their component parts.

The process of treating bows by heat was described in the eighteen-thirties by a Turk named Mustafa Kani, who wrote an excellent book on archery by command of the Sultan Mahmud II. Bows were dried in the sun or warmed over a fire, if too damp, in order to increase their cast but also, if the bow were too strong, it could be weakened by being baked in a felt-lined box for perhaps two days. The proper tempering to secure either result was evidently a matter of experience and judgment. Beyond stating that a heated bow should be hung in a cool, shady place before it is drawn, no hint is given of any other sort of conditioning in the many arid places—even deserts—where such bows were undoubtedly used.

2. LENGTH OF THE COMPOSITE BOW

The problem of the actual length of the composite bow of the Arabs is a baffling one. The span is given by most authorities as nine inches but, by actual measurement of hands, we have found that the average man can stretch his thumb and little finger not much over eight inches. If we accept the nine-inch span, the length of five one and a half spans would be sixty-seven and a half inches, and of five one and two thirds spans, seventy-five inches. The eight-inch span would give sixty-two and a half and seventy inches.

While such measurements would be quite acceptable for wooden bows, they certainly seem too long for the kind of Oriental composite bows of which we have seen examples, or have read about. And let us state at once that all our efforts to find a genuine Arab bow have so far been unsuccessful. We must form our opinions on comparisons, calculations, and a few questionable pictures.

The statement on page 77 of this volume, that "the length of the bow is three cubits and one finger," or sixty-five inches, agrees perfectly with the five-span measurements given above; yet how could one reconcile such a length with the statement on page 87 that "the arrow should measure exactly the length of the strung bow"? Evidently different sorts of bows were cited, the short ones being quite likely from Persian sources, or authors, and the long ones from Arabic.

The longest composite bow that we know of is the Chinese, which is seventy-four inches from end to end. However, such very long bows lose all the advantages that should be gained by composite structure and have a cast that is very poor in proportion to their weight: only a fraction of what the short Turkish and Persian bows can do.

As good specimens of short composite bows, we personally measured three beautiful ones from India that were exhibited in the Centennial Exhibition at Philadelphia in 1876. Their details are: Bow 1. Grip: 4 inches; arm: 10 inches; *siyah*: 9 inches. Total: 42 inches. Bows 2 and 3. Grip: 3½; arm: 9½; *siyah*: 6½. Total: 35½ inches.

The best Turkish bow of Sir Ralph Payne-Gallwey, author of *A Treatise on Turkish and other Oriental Bows* (1906), measured forty-four inches when unstrung and the bowstring was thirty-three inches in length, which would suggest a total strung length of perhaps a yard. A modern Sind bow in our collection, which is a masterpiece of bowyery in the ancient tradition, measures fifty-six inches.

In the Metropolitan Museum of Art are many Persian miniatures which show the composite bow very accurately: strung, and at full draw, but not, so far as I know, unstrung. Most of the bows that are strung, but at rest, are seen projecting from their quivers, which are hung on the right side of the archers exactly as described on page 155, but in a painting which is dated as prior to 1575 and is labeled: "Assad ibn Kariba attacks the army of Iraj suddenly by night," a very carefully limned archer holds a beautiful strung bow at rest. By measuring along its curvature with a fine flexible steel tape we found that its length was equal to the distance from the ground to the archer's nipple which, for a man of sixty-eight inches, would mean about fifty inches. It seemed to us that the assumption of accuracy in proportion was warranted.

Inasmuch as the Arab composite bow occupied an intermediate position between the Hijazite Arab and Persian bows, it was doubtless shorter than the former and longer than the latter. The direct statement that it measured sixty-five inches cannot be dismissed, especially in view of the great length of the arrows which is described in Section XXXVII.

Some collateral evidence is afforded by a Frenchman named Belon, writing in 1553—which is not so far from the date of the present manuscript—who said:

"The bows and quivers that the Arabs carry are different from the others of Turkey. The bows of the Arabs resemble more the Grecian bows than the Turkish bows, for the Turks of Asia carry a little bow well braced up, strongly curved, and very stiff. But the bows of the Cretans are of two sorts, of which those made in Sphagia [or Sphacteria, a small island off the southwest coast of Greece] with the horns of the ibex, and those made in Candia [Crete] with the horns of buffaloes, are larger than the Turkish; and since they are larger than the Turkish, so must they have long and thick arrows quite as much as the bows of the Arabs; for the Arabs have their bows big because it is necessary for them to use large arrows, contrary to the Turks, who have theirs small." (*Archers d'autre Fois*, Stein [Paris, 1925].)

3. THE COMPOSITE BOW

In order to find out the exact shape, size, and nature of the component parts of a composite bow, we dissected one of Chinese make by cutting cross sections at every inch. Fundamentally, we believe, all composite bows are built in the same general manner though they differ widely in pattern and materials. All of them are made

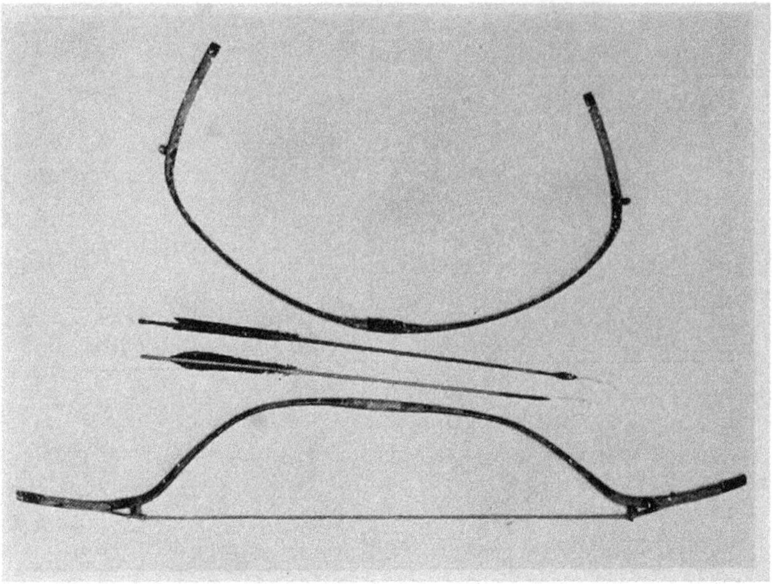

Above. Chinese Bow from Peking, Unstrung. *Below.* Similar Bow, Strung. Two Arrows from Canton

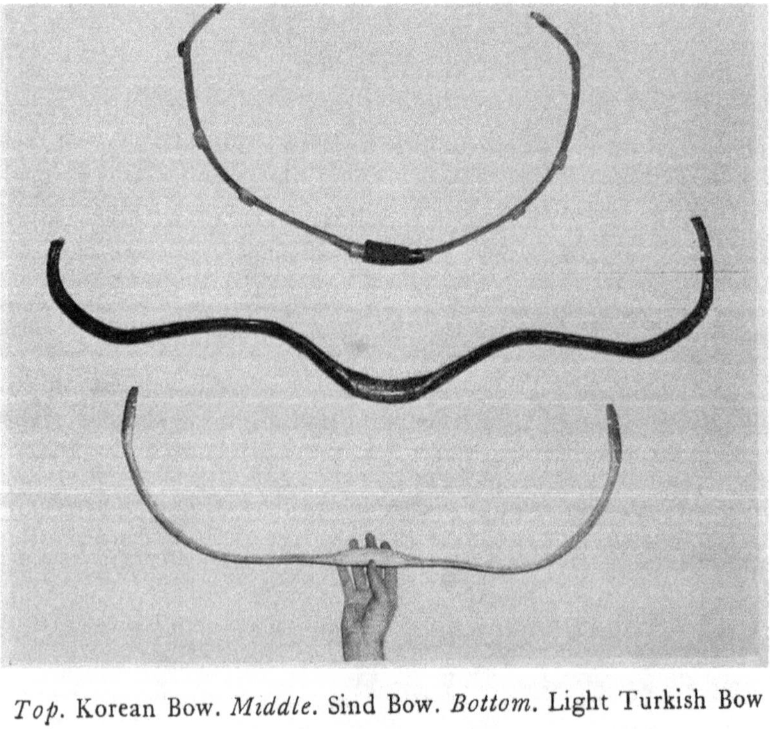

Top. Korean Bow. *Middle.* Sind Bow. *Bottom.* Light Turkish Bow

of a wooden core that is backed with sinew and bellied with horn.

In the English translation of Mustafa Kani's book, which came from the Turkish through the medium of German, the wood of the Turkish bow is said to be maple, which is used because it is particularly well suited to hold glue. The wood in our Chinese bow is of two kinds: unmistakable bamboo in the arms and a hard, close-grained wood in the *siyahs* and grip.

The sinews are probably the same for all bows and are taken from the legs and necks of various herbivorous beasts. Although they are molded with glue into a hard, compact mass, the fibers are often found to be surprisingly short if they are teased apart in hot water: anywhere from two inches to a foot or more.

We know of four kinds of horns that are used in composite bows. A crude Korean bow in our collection which is forty-eight and a half inches long, has two thin pieces of what looks like steer horn on each limb, spliced end to end for a total of ten inches. This is a poor and unusual material, however, for a prime requisite of the horn for bows should be that in its original state on the head it should have only a simple curvature in one plane—like the blade of a scythe—and not be twisted in other ways as in the case of cows or rams. Long strips are sawn from the upper and lower surfaces of such horns, but not from the sides, and corresponding pieces from the two horns of the same animal are mated in the two limbs of a bow.

The three horns which fulfill this requirement of simple curvature and are known to be used in composite bows are those of the carabao, the ibex, and certain species of the domestic goat. Although the ibex is a true goat and exists—always in a wild state—in the Near East and North Africa, we think that the "horn of goats" mentioned in the manuscript was taken from domestic animals.

In our Chinese bow the flat and wide strip of bamboo extends all the way from one *siyah* to the other and is joined to each by a single fish splice. The hard wood of the grip is simply glued onto the bamboo and merged into the flexible arm by gradual flattening. Kani says that in the Turkish bow the arm wood is spliced by a single fish to the grip as well as to the *siyahs*. The author of our text refers to these splices as the "sharp points" of the *siyahs* and grip.

In all composite bows that we know of, the sinew is carried in a continuous strip from *siyah* to *siyah*. At the grip—which is much narrower than the arms—it may be squeezed up into a ridge which the Arabs call the cockscomb and which provides a better hold for the fingers.

The *ibranjaq*—a word of otherwise undetermined meaning—is a piece of wood on the belly side of the grip which is accurately fitted between the ends of the two horns. Just why it is needed is problematical but, as all composite bows seem to have it in one shape or another, it is evidently necessary. Maybe it is a shock absorber.

In some, but not in all, composite bows, the grip is built out on the belly side to fit the palm of the hand. Whether this elevation was formed in the old Arab bow by the piece of bone called *khudrud*, or whether the *dustār* was a binding for some similar purpose, or whether both of those mysterious objects had other functions, is material for further research.

The kidney, or swelling above the grip—as seen in our Sind bow—seems to indicate a transverse binding of sinew to hold the three elements of the bow together at this point of greatest strain.

The neck is where the arm wood, the sinew, and the horn are attached to the *siyah*. It is the region of the splice.

The general meaning of *daffah* is something in the nature of a hinge.

One might wish, for simplicity, that the evolution of the composite bow had resulted in a nomenclature that was more in harmony with human anatomy. It is confusing to find the fingernail above the neck and the neck beside the knee.

4. BRACING

Correctly speaking, *stringing* means the fitting of a bare bow with a string, and *bracing* means flexing the bow thus fitted and slipping the eyes of the string into their nocks preparatory to shooting. *Bending*, incidentally, applies also to bracing the bow, not to drawing it. However, the author of our manuscript and nearly all modern archers use the word *stringing* as synonymous with *bracing*, and this practice we have followed in the translation.

All twelve methods of bracing that are described in this section are feasible for straight bows and for bows of moderate recurvature, but for Oriental bows that are so recurved—or reflexed—that when at rest they look like an inverted letter C, or an ellipsoidal loop, or even a pretzel, several of the methods would be practically impossible. The fact that all of them are offered in reference to the Arabic bow may be accepted as further evidence that that weapon was not as recurved as were many of the Turkish, Persian, or Asiatic Indian bows.

The easiest way to bend any rod is to press the ends in one direction and the center in the opposite, and that fundamental principle holds good for the bow. Therefore, all methods of bracing are merely different ways of applying force against the back of the bow near each tip and resisting that force, or making contrary pressure, at the grip.

The following synoptical scheme may help in understanding the twelve methods, all of which are reversible to right or left:

Method	*Position*	*Lower end*	*Grip*	*Upper end*
1	standing	left foot at ground	left hand, right knee	right hand
2	"	" " " "	left hand only	" "
3	"	left thigh-buttock groove	left hand	" "
4	"	ground	" "	" "
5	"	inside of leg	outside of thigh	" "
6	"	left hand	back	" "
7	sitting	" "	right hand	ground
8	" (assistant)	" "	knees	right hand
9	sitting (no assistant)	" "	"	" "
10	standing	front of thigh	back (vertical)	right hand behind head
11	kneeling, one knee	left hand	foot	right hand
12	sitting	left foot	both hands	right foot

The only method that seems hard to understand is number ten. To do it, the archer first steps into the bow with one leg—between the bow and the string. He then lays the bow down his back and brings the lower end out to the front between his legs, where it is hooked onto the thigh if the bow is a short one, or onto the shin if it is a long one. The bracing is then done by grasping the upper tip with one or both hands, either above or behind the head, and pulling it forward while the body inclines anteriorly from the hips. The shin, or thigh, and one or both hands control the two tips while the grip rests somewhere on the back. The upper eye slips in the nock easily. It is not nearly so hard as it sounds and is a good way to brace very heavy bows.

5. THE MALE FEATHER

The discovery of the *dhakar*, or male feather, is puzzling as well as surprising. On page 232 of the original manuscript—page 111 of this volume—it is clearly defined as a feather placed next to the arrowhead. In translating the passage Dr. Faris has taken the greatest pains and has reviewed his work repeatedly. If the description is true, the feather apparently stands away from the string just as the cock feather does on ordinary trifletched arrows, but instead of being fixed in the usual position with relation to the two side feathers—the three standing around the shaft 120 degrees apart—it is far up in front near the head. In this position, one might expect it to be stripped off by any penetrating shot.

Unfortunately, the anonymous author of our book is not as convincing as we could wish him to be, for his statement that "a certain author related that he had seen an expert" use the *dhakar* implies that he had never tried it himself and was citing from hearsay. Granting, for the moment only, that he was not in error, the sole use for such a vane which comes readily to mind would be for the steadying of a broadhead, which naturally presents more resistance to the air on its flat surfaces than on its sharp edges. Theoretically, such a feather might be expected to counteract side-slip, but all practical archers know that in actual shooting a broadhead goes very straight because the rotation of the arrow does not allow the head to remain in one plane.

However, inasmuch as this book never suggests that there were ever four feathers—the three normal feathers and the *dhakar*—we feel that it is not justifiable to accept the existence of an arrow fletched with two regular side feathers and a third—to us—abnormal feather near the head, but we believe that somewhere along the line of ancient scribes a description of the position of the cock feather was misinterpreted. Additional evidence is afforded by the fact that in the two other places where the *dhakar* is mentioned, that is, here on page 75 and on page 130, everything said of it would apply perfectly to a cock feather.

To test the action of an arrow with two side feathers and with another placed near the head, we constructed and shot such a missile. It wobbled and flirted just as we had expected it to do and proved, to our mind, that such an arrangement of fletching is not practicable.

6. THE CUBIT

It is a matter of high moment that the English equivalents of the Arabic weights and measures should be determined exactly, but the task is very difficult after so long a lapse of time and so many changes of standards. A surprisingly large number of measures used in the Orient have been called the cubit, and we cannot be categorical as to the one which was in the mind of our author. It is probable that the following citation indicates the cubit for which we are searching. It is abbreviated from the authoritative *Men and Measures* (1917) by Dr. Edward Nicholson, a British physician of wide Asiatic experience.

"Many centuries after the institution of the Assyrian great cubit of 25.26 inches, and of the Persian Beládi cubit of 21.88 inches, another important cubit became a standard of measure in the Moslem caliphate which reigned over the lands of the Eastern great kingdoms. Under Al-Māmūn, son of Harūn al-Rashid, science was flourishing in the East, while the West was in the dark ages, at least in all countries unenlightened by the civilization of the Moors in Spain. The cubit which was legally prescribed by Al-Māmūn was called the Black Cubit, and was so named from the black banner and dress adopted by the Abbaside caliphs.

"The Black Cubit equaled 21.28 inches and was derived from the common, or original, cubit of 18.24 inches as being equal to seven handbreadths of 3.04 inches whereas the latter is equal to six, thus:

Common Cubit = 18.24 = 6 × 3.04

Black Cubit = 21.28 = 7 × 3.04.

"This Black Cubit is still in use and is the basis of measures and of weights which spread from Egypt to every country in Europe. The old Nilometer (built 861 A.D.) on the island of Al-Rawḍah (the garden) has its cubits in this scale and measurements of the worn scale give 21.29 inches for the cubit."

We cannot ignore the fact, however, that the slightly longer cubit of 21.88 inches was also used in North Africa, as is attested by the following words from the same authority:

"The Persian cubit known as the Beládi (from *belád*, country) was one ten thousandth of a meridian league, or 21.88 inches. It passed to Spain with the Moors and is still found in the East."

The short cubit of 18.24 inches—also called the common cubit and original cubit—may probably be discarded by us because it seems to make the archery tackle too short for practical use, but we must confess that in some instances there is ample room for doubt.

In our calculations we will use the Black Cubit, which seems to figure out fairly well. However, in mathematical data our author is often far from modern standards of accuracy; for instance, he says that forty-five times three cubits and a finger equal one hundred and forty cubits, whereas they are obviously nearer to one hundred and thirty-seven cubits.

The approximate lengths given above will then be: 25 cubits = 14.8 yards; 125 cubits = 74 yards; 140 cubits = 82.75 yards; 300 cubits = 177.6 yards.

One bow-length = 65 inches (64.84); 45 bow-lengths = 81 yards.

7. WEIGHTS OF BOWS

The modern rotl is approximately equal to the English pound avoirdupois, except in some localities around the eastern shore of the Mediterranean where it varies from 3.93 to 6.35 pounds. These higher values can be eliminated at once from our consideration as they would give bows of absurd magnitude. It is almost certain, however, that the rotl referred to in the manuscript was equal to our pound troy and not to our pound avoirdupois. At that time it was the legal weight of Islam and was derived from the cubit of al-Ma'mūn, or Black Cubit, as follows:

Two-thirds of the Black Cubit of 21.28 inches gave the Black Foot of 14.186 inches. A cubic Black Foot of water weighed approximately 720,000 grains. This was divided for convenience into 125 parts of 480 grains each, called an *uqīyah*, which is the same as our troy ounce. Twelve *uqīyahs*, or troy ounces, made one rotl, or troy pound, of 5,760 grains. We will call it the Ancient Arabic rotl and base our calculations upon it.

The bow of 200 rotls has the greatest weight that is cited by the author. It is enough in itself to prevent us from adopting the modern rotl of one pound avoirdupois because a bow of 200 pounds is beyond ordinary human strength. Even by the Ancient Arabic rotl it would weigh 165 pounds. This is still indicative of an enormously strong bow which could be drawn only by men of gigantic strength and long training; yet there are recorded feats of Turkish archery which show that such athletes existed and some Turkish bows of nearly as great a weight are yet in existence. We must believe that such bows were actually used in Oriental warfare. In America, bows of about that strength have occasionally been shot by hand in competitive flight shooting, and bows up to 220 pounds have been shot—for distance only—by drawing with both hands against the feet; like rowing a boat, sitting down.

8. SIGHTING AND RANGE

The paragraph on page 79 suggests one very great advantage which lies in the Oriental manner of shooting past the right side of the bow; a technique which is possible only when the string is drawn by the thumb. When the arrow is shot past the left side of the bow, as is always the case in America, where the string is drawn by the tips of the fingers, a distant target is obscured by the bow hand. So, because the mark is thus hidden from his eye, the archer must aim empirically at something above it, like a tree, cloud, or hill. To avoid this source of inaccuracy, many archers now depart so far from the simple principles of pure archery as to affix a prismatic lens sight to the bow in order to bring the target into view by deflection. In the Oriental method all this is avoided and, as the text indicates, the archer can look at the target by direct vision between his fingers and can use them as an ascending or descending series of sighting levels.

We American archers must also remember that the Oriental draw was to the ear, or near it, and not to the chin or neck as with us. This gave a direct sight on the target at the short ranges, whereas in our method of holding the arrow lower than the eye, a sight over the arrowhead will fall on the ground if the shaft is in anything like a horizontal position.

The weight of the bow in this instance is 82 pounds, which is quite within reason, and the ranges of 300, 250, 200, 150, 100, 50, and 25 cubits are approximately equal to 177.6, 148, 113.6, 88.8, 74, 29.6 and 14.8 yards. However, the lay reader should realize that all such passages as these in the text, which purport to give the relations between weights and casts, are to be interpreted very loosely. Practical shooting is never as simple as such generalized rules would indicate. Bows may weigh exactly the same and yet vary enormously in their shooting qualities.

9. HORNS USED IN BOWS

The statement that five or six pieces should be contained in the horns of an extra heavy composite bow that is built for the one purpose of achieving the greatest length of cast—which means a competition, or flight, bow—is of both great importance and great obscurity, for the text does not tell us whether the pieces are to be laid in superimposed strata, or set end to end, or arranged in some other manner.

Composite bows that are backed with the horn of the carabao, or water buffalo, may not necessarily have more than one piece of horn in each arm so far as length is concerned, and as for thickness: the raw horn in its entirety as it comes from the head of the animal has such thick walls for most of its length that it would seem adequate for any bow. However, we are not certain that extra heavy bows may not need the reinforcement of a second layer, though we know of no direct evidence to that effect. At any rate, Mustapha Kani—in giving detailed instructions on how to saw strips of carabao horn—never mentioned more than a single strip from the top or bottom of the original horn, and gave no hint of its ever being reinforced by the addition of other layers.

The horn in our six-foot Chinese bows—which is undoubtedly carabao—is exposed to view without a wrapping and is twenty-four inches long in the upper limb and twenty-two in the lower. The horn in our fifty-five inch Sind bow is about sixteen inches in each limb, though it is hard to form a certain opinion because both limbs are entirely covered by what looks like painted and highly decorated parchment. Both horns seem to run into the four-inch grip and from end to end they measure about thirty-four inches—which, by the way, fits very well into the length of an arrow which is advised by "some others" on page 104. Halfway along each arm there is a concealed but indubitable wrapping of sinew which may be for the simple purpose of guarding against separation of the horn, wood, and sinew at that critical point, or may support a splicing of two pieces of horn.

We own a magnificent pair of carabao horns, from the Philippines, each of which measures thirty-four inches from root to tip; undoubtedly of a size and thickness that would do for any composite bow, but we have also seen half a ton of carabao horns that were imported from India by an American bowyer, and our impression was that perhaps a majority of them would not provide strips more than from eight inches to a foot in length that would be good enough for bows. It is obvious that strips as short as that would have to be spliced end to end to the number of from four to six in almost any sort of composite bow.

In the case of the Arab bow, however, we can discard the consideration of carabao horn because the manuscript states in several places that the horn was that of the goat. Angora goats and similar breeds that have spirally curled horns can be ruled out at once, however long their horns may be. The common goat that is found all around the Mediterranean coast has horns that satisfy the requirements for simple curvature, as we said on page 161, but they are not nearly as long as those of the carabao. Allowing for the pointed tip and scrawny base, the bowyer might find it hard to get satisfactory strips that were more than ten inches long and most horns probably would not yield that much.

The two pairs of slips, or strips, that make up the horn in our Korean bow, which look like steer but might be goat, add to twelve and a half inches in the upper limb and eleven in the lower; the two upper ones being seven inches each—joined by an overlapping splice of one and a half inches—and the lower being seven and six inches with an overlap of two inches. This difference in splicing would make it seem that the amount of overlapping was guided largely by convenience.

Goat horns being somewhat limited in length, on the average, it seems to us that the need for several pieces should not be at all unusual. In fact, if the Arab bow were "three cubits and a finger" in length, we hardly see how the use of multiple spliced pieces could be avoided. But the text specifies that the horns of the competition bow should be the width of two fingers shorter than the arrow and, on page 118, it defines the length of a competition arrow as nine fists. Assuming four inches for the fist, that would give an even yard for the length of the arrow and about thirty-four inches for the combined length of the two horns with their interposed *ibranjaq*. The *ibranjaqs* in Turkish bows are very narrow—about a quarter or half an inch—and if they were similar in Arab bows we can disregard them and consider each horn of the competition bow to have measured about seventeen inches. It seems doubtful to us that such long strips of horn could be cut in their entirety from a goat; they would have to be built up in the bow out of smaller pieces.

However, the inference derived from the text is that the sole purpose of using five or six pieces of horn in the competition bow is to make it stronger—meaning thicker, not longer—and this is confirmed by the statement that the arms should be round rather than flat. The arms of our dissected Chinese bow were each nine sixteenths of an inch in thickness, of which two sixteenths were sinew, four sixteenths wood, and three sixteenths horn—indubitably a single layer. The arms of our Sind bow are seven eighths, or nearly an inch, in thickness. If the proportions were similar to those in the Chinese bow the horn might be as much as five sixteenths of an inch thick. Remembering that our author has said, on page 88, that "the more horn it has the stronger it is," we may assume that a half inch of horn, or even more, would not be unreasonable.

As the horn slips in our Korean bow are only one sixteenth of an inch thick, five or six could be laid on top of each other without transcending acknowledged limits, but it would seem to be a foolish bowyer who would build up such an involved structure when he might use much larger pieces with better results and less difficulty. Besides, counting six laid for height and six spliced for length, the total would be thirty-six—a number which exceeds the bounds of credibility.

Why could there not be some such arrangement of pieces, for example, as two layers of three each with the splices of one layer set against the middle of the pieces of the other?

In the absence of the direct evidence which would be afforded by the dissection of a bow backed with goat horn, we may assume that the horny layer was sometimes built up of smaller elements than—before the translation of the present text—we had suspected were used, and that the arrangement of them was left to the bowyer.

To test these theories, we took the Sind bow to the hospital and had its spine X-rayed. Four pictures of the same portion were taken with varying technique but the results were not satisfactory because of the fact that some pigment—probably lead—greatly obscured the internal structure. Nevertheless, we could determine definitely that the horn and sinew each measured about three eighths and the wood about one quarter of an inch. We could not be certain that tapered splicing existed under the ligature of sinew but we thought we detected an oblique line which suggested it. In this, however, the hope of discovery may have taken command of the eye.

10. KNOTS

It is most unfortunate that the author did not describe the manner of tying these three knots, for we are now unable to prove exactly what they were. There are many kinds of knots on bows all over the earth but those which do not permit of quick and easy disengagement may be dismissed by us. Of the knot which the author calls Khurasanian, we have practically definite knowledge. We also have source proof of another knot which may be the *Ṣaʿdīyah*, or very near it. The Turkish knot still eludes us but we offer a rather poor possibility as being better than no guess at all.

We believe the Khurasanian to be what is usually known as the Asiatic Bowstring Knot, both because it fits the author's statement that it is the best and finest of all knots and because it seems always to have been used on composite bows. It is, in fact, ubiquitous over the whole continent of Asia. Some Chinese bowstrings in our possession are tied with it; the eyes being eight inches long so that the knots rest on the knees of the bow (see page 15). It is almost indispensable when the string is formed of fine strands, as of silken thread, which are strong in tensile stress but, because they are not adapted to withstand the friction of the bow nocks, must be supplemented by eyes made of some tough material like rawhide or thick cord of sinew or hemp. The body of such a string is really an endless skein of thread, and the knot is designed to join such widely different elements. To make it:

1. Hold the skein near the end with the left hand, making a loop in the form of a hairpin. 2. Take the piece to make the eye—a few inches in length—and bend it into a circle with overlapping ends. 3. Lay one of these overlapping ends on the front side of the loop and the other on the back. 4. Lead the front end around the side of the skein and push it from behind forwards through the loop; then lead the rear end around the other side and push it from before backwards through the loop. 5. Pull all taut.

It is interesting to observe here that we have never met a sailor who could tie this knot, and we have tested high officers of both the American and British navies as well as of the merchant marine, many of whom spent their early lives on sailing ships.

A knot that is used for strings of a single coarse material, like the camel's hide of the text, has been given us by Mr. Ingo Simon of England. We suggest it as the *Ṣa'dīyah*, though all we know definitely is that it was used by inhabitants of the Near East. To make it:

1. Tie a single knot, leaving several inches of free end. 2. Form the eye out of the free end. 3. Push the end through the upper aperture of the single knot on the opposite side of the cord. 4. Bend the end sharp around, thus embracing two strands of the single knot, and push it again through the upper aperture in the opposite direction. 5. Pull all taut.

The third knot that we offer is the Timber Hitch, which is really more of a slip noose than a knot and has to be loosened every time the bow is unstrung. While we do not claim that it is the Turkish knot which is mentioned in the text, it does have the attribute of being "good for coarse strings with weak bows because of the ease with which it is undone." In fact, it is incomparably more easy to undo than any other knot. In Europe and America, bowstrings that have one end furnished with an eye laid in the making and the other end left free invariably use this hitch to secure the free end. It is one of the best known knots and is described in most dictionaries. To make it:

1. Lead a short end of the bowstring around the string itself so as to form an eye. 2. Pass the free end back through this eye and wrap it twice around the far part of the string that forms the eye. 3. Set the eye in the bow nock and draw taut.

11. THE DIRHAM AND ITS EQUIVALENTS

The old Arabic dirham, according to Webster's and other dictionaries, equaled 45 English grains, and this weight seems to fulfill the requirements of the text of this book. On this basis the figures given on page 102 may be conveniently translated and tabulated as follows:

	Rotls	*Dirhams*	*Pounds*	*Grains*
Khurasanian	70	3, 3½	52½	135, 147½
	60	2, 2½	45	90, 112½
	30	1, 1½	22½	45, 67½
Persian	150	4	112½	180
	80	3	60	135
	70	3	52½	135
Some archers	200	5, 6, 8	150	225, 270, 360
	150	4½, 5	112½	202½, 225
	100	4½	75	202½
	90	3, 3½, 4	67½	135, 147½, 180
	80	Same	60	Same
	70	Same	52½	Same
Competition bow	100	2, 3	75	90, 135

The weight of an average American string made of linen thread is about 150 grains, with considerable variation.

12. LENGTHS OF ARROWS

The following measurements are taken from a man of average height—about sixty-nine inches:

Length of foot	10.5 inches	Forearm	11 inches
Height of foot	2.75 "	Chest	18 "
Leg, inner side	31.5 "	Fist	3.75 "

Arrows calculated on these data would be:

Abu-Hāshim	Cubit & forearm	33 inches
	Leg & foot	34.25 or 42
	Leg & forearm	42.5
	Chest & forearm	29
Ṭāhir	Armpit to finger tip	29
Others	8 to 12 fists	30, 33.75, 37.5, 41.25, 45

Indefinite as are these crude measurements, they still teach us that the Oriental arrows which were shot in the normal or original manner, that is, without a guide that would permit a short arrow to be drawn beyond the bow, were fully as long as those which were used in medieval England or are still used in China and Japan. The English standard war arrow, or "livery arrow," was probably about 30 inches in length, with variations up to the 37 inches of the cloth-yard shaft. There may also have been a reduction of one or two inches for short archers, although the ancient practice of drawing to the ear permitted control of a greater length than does the modern draw to, or under, the chin. Both the Chinese and Japanese sometimes use very short arrows for special purposes, but their usual arrows that we have seen vary from about 35 to 37 inches. We have seen many very diminutive Japanese archers draw these long shafts full to the arrowhead, which they do by bringing the right hand well back of the ear. Arrows of a five foot length or more are used in South America and Polynesia but they are never drawn for more than a convenient portion of the shaft, a custom which was apparently never followed by the Arabs.

Drawing with the thumb gives a two or three inch advantage over drawing with the finger tips; so that the American who can handle a 28 inch arrow could use one of 30 or 31 inches if he drew with that kind of hold, and he could add considerably more if he drew to his ear. So far as length of shaft is concerned, the Asiatics had, and still have, a double advantage over us.

It is reasonable to surmise that the average Oriental arrow of the unabbreviated type measured from about 29 to 34 inches and that longer and shorter ones were also known and used.

13. RELATIVE WEIGHTS

If we accept the *uqīyah* as equal to our troy ounce of 480 grains (see page 166), then this dirham would weigh 43.2 grains, which is near enough—for the practical calculations of archery—to the 45 grain dirham which we have already used. If anyone wishes to refine the results still further, for his own satisfaction, he must bear in mind that all those old weights showed minor variations.

We believe that the barley mentioned by the author was the barley seed still in its husk. To test his text, we weighed fifty-one American barleycorns of local growth—using samples from two farms. When dry, they weighed only twenty-four grains and, even after swelling them up by soaking in water overnight, the most we could get was a weight of thirty-seven grains.

There are many strains of barley in the world and it is possible—though we have no evidence one way or the other—that the barley of ancient Morocco may have been larger than ours and that fifty and two-fifths corns did, in fact, weigh from forty-three to forty-five grains. If they did not weigh that much, the dirham of our translation may be heavier than the one the author had in mind.

Here are some of the relative weights of bows, arrows, and parts of arrows as they are given in this section (the pounds being avoirdupois):

Various archers										
	Bow	20	rotls,	16.5	pounds;	arrow	3	dirhams,	135	grains
	"	30	"	25	"	"	4	"	180	"
	"	80—	"	66—	"	"	7	"	315	"
	"	80	"	66	"	"	10	"	450	"
	"	over 100	"	over 82	"	"	16-20	"	720-900	"
Tāhir	"	Stiff		?		"	12	"	540	"
	"	30	"	25	"	"	8 1/3	"	375	"
	"	40	"	33	"	"	"	"	"	"
	"	50	"	41	"	"	"	"	"	"
	"	60	"	49	"	"	10	"	450	"
	"	90	"	74	"	"	"	"	"	"
	"	100	"	82	"	"	12-16	"	540-720	"

Parts of arrow

Arrow	7 dr.	315 gr.	Wood	255 gr.	Head 45 gr. Glue and Feathers 15 gr.
"	10 "	450 "	"	383 "	Head, Glue, and Feathers 67.5 gr.
"	7 "	315 "	"	264 "	Head 45 gr. Feathers 6.5

The last line gives the "first ratio." For the second and third ratios the author seems to be exhibiting a tendency toward excessive meticulosity.

14. THE *majra* OR ARROW GUIDE

The description, on page 126, of the *majra*, or arrow guide, and its uses, is one of the most important discoveries in modern toxophilitic research. So far as we know, the *majra* has never been mentioned elsewhere in the English language, and its presence here resurrects a fact of gripping interest which had been lost in the oblivion of time.

Until now, the only arrow guide of which we had any knowledge was the kind which we will designate by its Turkish name of *siper*. This has been well studied by Dr. Paul E. Klopsteg of Chicago, who partially described it in his book *Turkish Archery* (1934), and who, in the light of accumulated knowledge, expects to write on it at much greater length in the near future.

The *siper* is a thin piece of horn, bone, tortoise shell, or other hard substance, about six inches long, one inch wide, slightly convex in its longitudinal axis, and grooved about one quarter of an inch deep for its whole length. These measurements are, however, subject to considerable variation. Attached to its bottom is an ingenious harness, usually of leather or silk, by which it is fastened to the bow-hand and held above the thumb on the right side of the bow. To protect the bow-hand in case the arrow should jump out of the groove, a flat, elliptoid piece of leather or other suitable material is slipped between the *siper* and hand harness, a slot being cut in it for that purpose. One can therefore see that the *siper* is a fixed, immovable support for the arrow which is contrived to let the archer engender greater force by enabling the bowstring to be drawn further than the length of the arrow would normally permit. However, it may not project more than about half a foot from the belly without getting in the way of the string and, for that reason, it cannot reduce the length of an available arrow by more than that amount. For example, a thirty inch draw would require an arrow of about twenty-five and a half inches, which is, in fact, the real length of many extant Turkish shafts. Obviously, a shorter arrow would fall off the hind end of the *siper*; nor can any other kind of short missile be used with a *siper* unless it be carried loosely in the hollowed end of a longer arrow, or shaft, that is fastened to the bowstring.

The *majra* discloses the entirely different principle of a long grooved trough with the bowstring sliding along its surface. Although it is freely movable—in contradistinction to the *siper*—it is the undoubted ancestor of the crossbow; an hypothesis which is substantiated by the following passage taken from page 12 of this book:

"The Turks and most of the Persians make this bow heavy, and set it on a *majra*, which they fit with lock and trigger and to the end affix a stirrup, thus making it a foot bow."

The text of our manuscript shows the typical *majra* to be a thin, grooved stick, possibly twice as thick as the arrow and about three inches longer, which rests and slides on the bow-hand just as an arrow does, but is not shot away like an arrow because it is not nocked to the string and because it is tied to the ring finger of the right hand by a short cord. Within the groove, the arrow is laid and nocked to the string. For this act the bow is canted enough to keep the arrow from falling out but, in practice, we have found that the inclination need not be very great. Although all the directions refer to its use on the right side of the bow, over the thumb of the bow-hand, it can be used just as well on the left side with the European finger draw.

The near end of the *majra* is sharpened like a pen, but not like a pencil; that is, it is left flat on top to make contact with the nock of the arrow but is sharpened on the sides and bottom to form a convenient hold. The groove of the *majra* should be ample enough to let the arrow slide without undue friction. At the penlike end the floor of the groove may be raised a trifle and the sides brought in enough to fit the nock end of the arrow accurately so that when the *majra* and arrow are pressed together by the clench, or lock, the cock feather within the groove cannot act as a fulcrum and raise up the shaft. The most satisfactory one of our homemade *majras* was thirty inches long and three quarters of an inch wide, with a squared three-eighths inch groove.

To use a *majra*:

1. Lay it across the bow like an arrow, resting on the bow-hand or thumb—that is, whether in European or Oriental style—with the near end just past the string so as not to get nocked by accident, and with the groove away from the bow. It must be held temporarily by the index finger of the bow-hand or it will fall off.
2. Cant the bow and lay the arrow in the groove, nocked to the string with a tight fit. The index finger must hold both arrow and *majra* in place.
3. Treat the united arrow and *majra* as a single unit, clenching and drawing them together in the usual manner.
4. Loose as usual. Now the short arrow, or other missile, flies out of the *majra* with amazing speed, while the *majra* itself remains behind.

Those are the essential features of the operation, but all the details of technique mentioned in the manuscript are of value, even to the gymnastics of twirling the *majra* around the head.

15. MEANING OF *fard* AND *qīrāṭ*

Believing that the only way to interpret the very involved description on page 135 with intelligence was to learn to do the stunt, we became sufficiently proficient at it to feel that we had cleared up its more salient mysteries.

Before explaining the process, let us look at those Arabic words: *fard* and *qīrāṭ*. It appears that they must have had some special meaning that was understood by contemporary archers because they can hardly be translated literally in the present context. According to the best Arabic-English dictionary, *fard* means: "single, as opposed to double; odd, as opposed to even." *Qīrāṭ* is the predecessor of our word "carat," and is a measure of weight equal to four grains; but, according to Webster's dictionary—cited under *carat*—it may also mean a bean. One is inclined to jump to the conclusion that they stood for any small object such as a modern archer might use to indicate a point of aim, but closer scrutiny does not prove that the parallel is exact. Here it may be fitting to explain to the lay reader the meaning of that expression. An archer can seldom sight the tip of his arrow directly at the target because the arrow is always on a slant and is not level like the barrel of a gun; so he picks out something else to sight at—either above or below the target—which he thinks will give the correct trajectory, and that object is then known as his point of aim. When this point is on the ground, he may use some natural feature, such as a tuft of grass, or, in target shooting, he may put some small but conspicuous gadget in the right place. The *fard* or *qīrāṭ* would certainly correspond to this if the archer sighted the tip of his arrow in line with it but, apparently, the Arab set one of them, or even his own foot, on the ground more with the purpose of using it to assist his judgment—as one will look at the object at which he throws a stone.

To perform the difficult feat, one must remember to shoot in the Arabic way, with the arrow on the right side of the bow and a thumb lock of sixty-three. Draw the arrow half its length, as the text prescribes. At this moment there occur those unusual movements which put this type of shooting into the category of stunts. The right hand is swung over and behind the head till the arm or wrist lies back of the neck. This could not be done if the position of the left hand were not altered during the movement because, if the string remained in its natural position, it would be caught in the armpit. Therefore, the bow-hand must be turned outward with a complete reversal of the bow so that the upper limb points backward, the lower limb points forward, and the palm is away from the body holding the bow in a horizontal position. The string then rides clear outside of the arm and can be drawn up as high as one wishes. From here on, the bow is not drawn but is pushed, as the right hand is fixed behind the neck and cannot move; so a full extension to the length of the arrow is obtained by straightening the left arm. It is then quite easy and natural to look down at the toe, or ground, or at whatever the *fard* or *qīrāṭ* might be, and to loose the arrow with confidence and a good aim. The length of the reach that is afforded by this method of shooting adds considerable evidence in support of the thesis that the Arabian arrow was much longer than ours. We found that at least a thirty-four inch shaft was desirable and a cloth-yard shaft could be handled with ease. As the author intimates, the strain is very great and a soft, or weak, bow is advised.

16. THE RETURNING ARROW

While the Arabic adjective that describes this arrow is correctly translated as "returning," the temptation to use the word *boomerang* was very strong. That such an arrow was also known to the English appears from the following quotation of a footnote on page 163 of *The English Bowman* (London, 1801) by T. Roberts, "a member of the Toxophilite Society" and an acknowledged authority:

"It is said, that if a light shaft is feathered at *both ends*, the wood being lightest at the pile-end and the feather trimmed low at the nock-end and high at the pile-end, and shot against the wind, that it will *return back again*. And, that a shaft feathered in the *middle* will, in its flight, make a *right angle*."

We made an arrow very carefully on the Arabic plan: cutting nocks in both ends, making a hole at the bottom of one nock and filling it with solder, and trimming it with low feathers at the nock end and high feathers at the pile end—though there was no pile. The only oversight was that we used six feathers instead of eight. Whether or not the difference of two feathers was the factor that caused the disappointing action of the arrow we do not know but, though shooting it repeatedly and against a very light wind, we could not make it return. The graceful sweep like that of a soaring buzzard which we had hoped for was not even suggested. What invariably happened was that the arrow would go much as usual for about forty yards from a forty-six pound osage bow of good cast and then would turn over, flutter indefinitely with an almost complete loss of force, and fall to the earth nock end first with just enough momentum to stick up. We agree perfectly with the author that it did not return to the place where we were standing because we were not exact in its construction. The arrow certainly reversed itself on every flight and lost practically all forward motion, and we are inclined to believe that if it were properly designed it might swing around in a great arc back to the point of departure instead of becoming tangled up in its own conflicting forces and falling in impotence. However, we felt certain that the averred use of such an arrow to shoot an unsuspicious enemy, who was standing at the archer's side, was no more than an untested bit of romantic fancy.

During the same experiments we tried shooting an arrow that was feathered in the middle and found that it did exactly what was expected of it. From the same bow it would also fly straight for about forty yards and then would turn at a right angle with apparently very little diminution of speed. There seemed to be no obvious way of controlling the direction of its altered course. Shot from the left of the bow it might turn straight down into the earth, fly off to the right, or go in any other direction. We finally lost it when it sped off toward the left in a high, wide, and handsome course at right angles to its original line of flight and cut through the leaves of the tall forest like a swift and reckless bird. It was fun.

17. FEATHERLESS ARROWS

Al-Ṭabari was right! We have in our possession two featherless arrows which exactly fit the description on page 140, except that they taper in the rear half but not at all in the fore half. They are twenty-five inches long, seven sixteenths of an inch in diameter in the thick part and taper to one quarter of an inch near the nock. The nock is bulbous, being almost a sphere nine sixteenths of an inch in diameter, with a slot one quarter of an inch wide and three sixteenths deep. The wood is about as heavy and strong as birch but is concealed by rings of red, yellow, green and black paint.

These are modern arrows used by the Sinds of India for the very purpose and in the same way that is ascribed to al-Ṭabari. They were given to us by Major J. B. Farley of England, who had spent most of his life in government service in India. He also gave us the magnificent modern composite bow—a powerful weapon—with which they were shot but, unfortunately, in our steam-heated house the bow developed a crack which made it useless for shooting.

The technique of the Sinds was to hold the bow in a horizontal position near the ground and place the arrow on the string at an angle; that is, with the nock several inches above the normal nocking point, so that the arrow received a side thrust as well as a forward thrust and, consequently, whirled around like a pinwheel while it went forward only a few yards. The idea seemed to be to knock the bird down without shedding its blood. Major Farley commented on the great waste of force in using such strong bows to shoot in a manner that would carry such a little distance and so feebly. We have never seen any other arrows like these in museums or elsewhere and believe that they are quite rare specimens in this country, if not unique.

The feathered type of sidewise arrow seems to have been of a different nature. If the nock end were heavy enough with relation to the pile end and the feathers were small, it could be shot sidewise for a short cast if nocked at an angle, but it would not do as much revolving nor would it travel in a straight line.

INDEX

CPSIA information can be obtained
at www.ICGtesting.com
Printed in the USA
BVHW071142210121
598322BV00004B/449

9 781614 279242